A Literary Christmas

SELECTED ESSAYS

A Literary Christmas

SELECTED ESSAYS

Various Authors

A Literary Christmas: Selected Essays

ISBN-13: 978-1-62834-023-5

ISBN-10: 1-62834-023-1

Table of Contents

Preface

What is the meaning of Christmas? Quiz a variety of individual persons on their notions of Christmas and the answers may reveal a kaleidoscopic variety of perspectives and opinions, memories and traditions. Although perhaps few take the time to pause and reflect on the deeper meaning of the busy season of family gatherings, holiday parties and concerts, gift-shopping and tree decorating, "A Literary Christmas," provides some food for thought. These descriptive accounts and articulate discussions have been carefully drawn by the pens of American authors and published in the pages of American and English magazines. The cultural traditions of Christmas in America and those borrowed from Europe, in wartime or in times of peace, in religious and secular life, show the deep roots of Christmas within the social fiber of American life.

From *The Bookman* magazine, valuable selections include "The Story of the Christmas Story," by Edna Kenton, who looks at the growing popularity of Christmas-themed short stories, inspired by the example of Charles Dickens; "The Story of a Christmas Story," by Henry Litchfield West," takes a different look at Dickens' famous "Christmas Story," its various editions and its role in the mass commercialism of Christmas; Annie Russell Marble's essay, "Christmas Carols, Ancient and Modern," traces the roots of popular Christmas carols and songs; "The Passing of the Christmas Ghost Story," by Stephen Leacock, talks about the multiplication of

Christmas ghost stories following Dickens' example; "The Christmas Crèche and the Passion Play," by Amelia Von Ende, describes a collection of Nativity scenes on display at a museum in Germany.

The story of the three Magi, the Wise Men who came from the East, is retold by A. Hilliard Atteridge, in the January 1885 issue of *The Month* magazine, along with a discussion in favor of a Persian origin of the three mysterious persons whose relics were spirited away to Europe in the early centuries of Christianity.

Other Christmas-themed articles excerpted from *The Century Magazine, The North American Review, The Outlook,* as well as the British magazine, *The Gentleman's Magazine,* combine to present a comprehensive look at the Christmas holiday and how it is celebrated at home in America and abroad.

The Story of the Christmas Story.

BY EDNA KENTON

From "The Bookman," December 1910

It was Christmas Eve. My old friend, Jack Vincent, had persuaded me to join him in the festivities at his father's country house"; so speeds the opening fire of the Christmas society tale. "The winter wind is howling over the bleak moor, and Christmas is ushered in with a sore famine that has already made many a hearth desolate"; this for the angry landlord plot! "I don't suppose you air going' to do much Christmas over to your house" — rural New England — or perhaps Tennessee Mountains, or the mining camp! "It was Christmas Eve. The heavy clouds, lowering all day, had wrapped the earth in a dun grey blanket that chilled the flesh and the spirit"; so begins the story that may be placed anywhere and treat of anything!

And harking back to the middle of the last century, the time when periodical literature first began to take notice of concrete rather than abstract things, it is apparent that the Christmas stories of 1910, like the Christmas stories of 1900 and of 1890, bear, most of them, the stale bouquet of an ancient vintage, or, to change the metaphor, they are *réchaufées* from bases scores of years old. And still the world demands them for food and drink in December, or, if it does not, the editorial fraternity is self-deceived beyond words.

THE STORY OF THE CHRISTMAS STORY

Christmas stories in the form of folk fables, songs, and traditions, have existed in literature for hundreds of years, but the Christmas story, as the modern world knows it, is probably not a hundred years old. Washington Irving, in his *Sketch Book*, published about 1820, was the notable pioneer in employing Christmas myths frankly as literary material. *The Sketch Book* was warmly received in England, and this American influence, combined with a strong fancy for the German holiday *Annuals* that sold in England for a good many years, gave the impetus to a literary movement that culminated in the "Christmas Books" of Dickens and Thackeray. This period, from 1842 to 1855, was the heyday of the Christmas story in literature. It attained to the dignity of many books on whose title pages were inscribed the two greatest names then known in English fiction. The literary world has not seen the like before or since. It is doubtful if such honor to any single human tradition will ever be paid again. But beginning with the middle of the nineteenth century the Christmas story has played an important part in periodical literature, and has been bound within permanent covers oftentimes far more worthy of preservation than their contents. It is to periodical literature, however, that one turns instinctively in seeking the story of the Christmas story, for the theme is difficult of sustained treatment, and finds its suitable place in that convenient depository of brevities, the monthly magazine.

In the leisurely days of the past mid-century that will probably never come again until the earth and its people are dying together, the Christmas story came, if it came at all, after Christmas. In February, 1853, *Harper's Magazine* composedly published "Christmas Stories" by a writer named Charles Dickens. In *Blackwood's Magazine* for January, 1857, splendidly placed between the scientific leader, "New Facts and Old Fancies about Sea Anemones" and the muckraker article "Routine," is the timely short story of the month, "A Christmas Tale!" And until far into the '70's the January numbers limped along, freighted with a belated Christmas spirit.

But piping modern days have changed all this mightily. Yellow

10

journalism in the '80's so infected conservative periodicals with the tyrannical germ of "timeliness" that, with the advent of the '90's and the cheaper magazines, there was a string among the dry bones of "Tables of Contents," and Christmas tales came to be printed promptly in December numbers. But the December magazines did not then make their bows on the first and the tenth and the fifteenth of November. Now, at best, we must read of Christmas joys before the Thanksgiving turkey has browned, and were we a Thanksgivingless nation the November magazines would have been filled probably long since with all the holiday rehash of fact and fancy that the world, being given, accepts with the docility that distinguishes the masses under unquestioned leadership. As it is, at least one Christmas tale of 1910 saw the Thanksgiving number and went it one month better, for last October one magazine published after the flare of a September advertisement a story than which none was ever built more openly upon the Christmas plot.

This, however, is a hopeful sign, in that we may take it to mean that there is a growing tendency to break away from the mass of inconsequent variations on the single December theme, and to make up the December program on more varied lines than in the immediate past. For there was a decade, beginning somewhere in the '90's, during which the American magazines — and English ones, too, for that matter — went fairly mad in the December numbers. The magazine cover came into its own then, and the newsstands were blatant with gold and silver and red and green inks. Within these bedizens covers Christmas art and Christmas fiction and Christmas myths and customs — and Christmas poetry alas! — ruled the pages. The Virgin beamed or sorrowed from every pictured leaf, and the reading matter confirms the gloomy suspicion that in those days the illustrations were articled rather than the articles illustrated. And during this period in particular the perennial short-story writers brought forth — by most of their fruits one is smitten with the memory of the straining mountain's mothering of the mouse — the sad or sweet, or sad and sweet, Christmas story.

And the plots of the Christmas stories, then and now! Art, said Whistler in effect, is art, only all traces of the machinery that has produced it are eliminated. The Christmas plot machinery sticks up from the surface of the Christmas story like a sore thumb on a workingman's hand. The lost child — found on Christmas Day! "And unto them a child was given!" The fatal quarrel — and on this theme may be written as many stories as there are human relationships — the reconciliation on Christmas Day: "Peace on earth!" And all the rest of the familiar contrivances.

The inevitable happened, of course, after years of this retailing of threadbare material. Not too many such December numbers were needed to rouse the sense of humor in some writers' breast, who began to play with Christmas plots. Frank Stockton did this deliciously in many of his Christmas stories. John Kendricks Bangs turns the same trick in a seemingly desperate effort to preserve his self-respect and to deliver the annual tale. George Ade, in "Mr. Payson's Satirical Christmas," takes a similar line on the Christmas plot, though in the end that tale approximates closely the inevitable annual.

Years ago Frank Stockton wrote "Stephen Skarridge's Christmas." It begins thus: "'Twas Christmas Eve. An adamantine sky hung dark and heavy over the earth," and Arthur Tyrrell, a clerk of Skarridge's, gazing sadly upon his wife and two children, sallied forth with but ten cents to buy their Christmas dinner. He returned with an eight-cent mackerel — happy Mr. Tyrrell who lived before the cost of living must have killed him! — and returned him followed by his harsh and miserly landlord, who, failing his rent, took away the mackerel. That night Skarridge, in his study, sees three ghosts, the mackerel, the fairy, and the giant. Ensues his conversion, and he sallies forth to make amends to the Tyrrells. He showers turkeys, geese, ducks, pickles and pie upon them. Also a farm, bonds and cash. Then, "with an arm about the neck of the still young, once beautiful, and now fast improving Mrs. Tyrrell, Skarridge stood, hounded by memories of the past — Did you ever before read a story like this?"

Now when ridicule comes in, sentimentality steps out, and pallid imitations of old Scrooge and his Ghosts cannot be published side by side with Stephen Skarridge and his mackerel-eyed spirit. The likeness is too plain. Stockton did not believe simplicity in Skarridge's conversion — neither do the re-creators of Scrooge hold him to kneel at a real mourner's bench. Conditions have changed, and with them the standpoints of men. The world is a little better able to face the truth of environments, and the batter of the typical Christmas story with its fluff of sentiment and the "happy ending" added last is too unsubstantial to rise and hold its own against the heavy atmospheric pressure of modern realism. The times themselves no longer breed men who can write of Scrooge and his Ghosts with such sincere faith in the old villain's story-book conversion as to inspire in the reader, if not faith in Scrooge's new leaf, an earnest if only temporary desire to be converted himself. The abiding power of *A Christmas Carol* lies in its compelling conviction of its author's faith in his puppets — and latter-day authors do not believe in puppets, even though they employ them constantly. This lack of faith on the part of the modern manipulators of the Christmas Punch and Judy shows is one of the reasons why the modern Christmas story is usually a bore.

The modern method has stepped in, of course, and has saved a number of Christmas stories. Mary E. Wilkins-Freeman has written a few in which the New England psychology is entirely worthwhile, and is plausibly stirred into action by the spirit of the chosen time. Katharine Holland Brown has a little boy, *Dawn*, which was published first, by the way, in an August fiction number, and which has never been advertised as a Christmas story. Primarily it is the tale of how a physician, nerve-racked and shaken for months, "comes back" under the compelling power of another's lonely need, and, in the dawn of Christmas Day, looks in wonder at the steady hand that had wrought the miracle of life the night before. But it is worth almost any hundred of the ordinary Christmas stories. And William J. Locke has just out a charming little tale, *Three Wise Men*, modern to a degree with its incidental references to radium and helium, thorium and argon of which Sir Angus McCurdie, physicist, knows the latest word. Biggleswade, the Assyriologist, and the Right Honorable Viscount Doyne, Empire builder and Administrator, make up the group of embodied wisdom which, in a lonely hovel, is brought face to face with the commonest phenomenon and the greatest mystery of the universe, and before it stands ignorant. There comes out of Death, Life, and, to the three childless, embittered men, a son. Save for one unnecessary line it is a tale not for one day in the year, but for all the year. Almost all of the ponderous Christmas machinery is taken away, and yet the spirit of Life and Love and Reconciliation and Peace is there. For a final example of the modern Christmas story, we may merely mention James Lane Allen's uncompleted trilogy, psychological to a degree, with the Christmas tree and the mistletoe standing for any and everything but what they banally signify. It is wiser to wait for the final volume before asserting Mr. Allen's failure or success.

But on the whole, the Christmas story is vanishing. For fifty years and more it has flared in the winter skies. But the sentiment that made possible that annual Christmas labor of writers like Dickens and Thackeray has evaporated somehow in the press of the modern world. A good many people are coming to look upon the holidays in somewhat the same manner that psychologists regard religious revivals, as a purely temporary and rather regrettable cerebral excitement, even for the children to whom they would wholly dedicate the day. The magazine excitement, too, has decreased in the last few years, and except for the more than timely cover designs, and always excepting the women's magazines, they are fairly as they are made up in the other months of the year. One or two Christmas stories, of course, and fillers of Christmas poetry; but the Madonnas are not being reprinted every year now, and the intense editorial interest in the church-art education of the masses has gratefully calmed down.

Again, with the exception of the women's magazines there are few encyclopedic articles on "Christmas Customs in Other Lands" and like dead subjects, because humanity is becoming interested in humanity at last, and seeks to know not so much of its merry-makings as of its civic and working conditions. The nations are slowly growing up, and the magazines and their editors are, a little more slowly, growing up with them. And since the Christmas story is essentially a beautiful fairy tale for children in their grown-up moods or for adults in their childish ones, enough have already been written to survive, and more than enough of the weaker that must perish. That there is always room for a masterpiece goes without saying.

The Stage-Coach.

BY WASHINGTON IRVING

From 'The Voyage
and Other English Essays,' 1820

Omne bené
Sine poenâ
Tempus est ludendi.
Venit hora
Absque morâ
Libros deponen.

OLD HOLIDAY SCHOOL SONG.[1]

In the preceding paper I have made some general observations on the Christmas festivities of England, and am tempted to illustrate them by some anecdotes of a Christmas passed in the country; in perusing which, I would most courteously invite my reader to lay aside the austerity of wisdom, and to put on that genuine holiday spirit which is tolerant of folly and anxious only for amusement.

In the course of a December tour in Yorkshire, I rode for a long distance in one of the public coaches, on the day preceding Christmas. The coach was crowded, both inside and out, with passengers who, by their talk, seemed principally bound to the

---

1   The stanza signifies that it is well there is a time for making merry that brings no punishment, and that the hour is at hand for promptly putting aside one's books.

mansions of relations or friends, to eat the Christmas dinner. It was loaded also with hampers of game, and baskets and boxes of delicacies; and hares hung dangling their long ears about the coachman's box, presents from distant friends for the impending feast. I had three fine rosy-cheeks schoolboys for my fellow passengers inside, full of the buxom health and manly spirit which I have observed in the children of this country. They were returning home for the holidays, in high glee, and promising themselves a world of enjoyment. It was delightful to hear the gigantic plans of the little rogues, and the impracticable feats they were to perform during their six weeks' emancipation from the abhorred thralldom of book, birch, and pedagogue. They were full of the anticipations of the meeting with the family and household, down to the very cat and dog; and of the joy they were to give their little sisters, by the presents with which their pockets were crammed; but the meeting to which they seemed to look forward with the greatest impatience was with Bantam, which I found to be a pony, and, according to their talk, possessed of more virtues than any steed since the days of Bucephalus.[2] How he could trot! How he could run! And then such leaps as he would take — there was not a hedge in the whole country that he could not clear.

They were under the particular guardianship of the coachman, to whom, whenever an opportunity presented, they addressed a host of questions, and pronounced him one of the best fellows in the world. Indeed, I could not but notice the more than ordinary air of bustle and importance of the coachman, who wore his hat a little on one side, and had a large bunch of Christmas greens stuck in the buttonhole of his coat. He is always a personage full of mighty are and business, but he is particularly so during this season, having so many commissions to execute in consequence of the great interchange of presents. And here, perhaps, it may not be unacceptable to my untraveled readers, to have a sketch that may serve as a general representation of

---

2   The favorite charger of Alexander the Great. Tradition tells how Alexander, in his boy-
    hood, tamed Bucephalus, thus fulfilling the condition stated by an oracle as necessary
    for obtaining the throne of Macedon.

this very numerous and important class of functionaries, who have a dress, a manner, a language, an air, peculiar to themselves, and prevalent throughout the fraternity; so that, wherever an English stage-coachman may be seen, he cannot be mistaken for one of any other craft or mystery.

He has commonly a broad, full face, curiously mottled with red, as if the blood had been forced by hard feeding into every vessel of the skin; he is swelled into jolly dimensions by frequent potations of malt liquors, and his bulk is still further increased by a multiplicity of coats, in which he is buried like a cauliflower, the upper one reaching to his heels. He wears a broad-brimmed, low-crowned hat; a huge roll of colored handkerchief about his neck, knowingly knotted and tucked in at the bosom; and has in summer time a large bouquet of flowers in his button-hole, the present, most probably, of some enamored country lass. His waistcoat is commonly of some bright color, striped, and his small-clothes extend far below the knees, to meet a pair of jockey boots which reach about halfway up his legs.

All this costume is maintained with much precision; He has a pride in having his cloths of excellent materials, and, notwithstanding the seeming grossness of his appearance, there is still discernible that neatness and propriety of person, which is almost inherent in an Englishman. He enjoys great consequence and consideration along the road; has frequent conferences with the village housewives, who look upon him as a man of great trust and dependence; and he seems to have a good understanding with every bright-eyed country lass. The moment he arrives where the horses are to be changed, he throws down the reins with something of an air, and abandons the cattle to the care of the hostler; his duty being merely to drive from one stage to another. When off the box, his hands are thrust into the pockets of his great coat, and he rolls about the inn bar with an air of the most absolute lordliness. Here he is generally surrounded by an admiring throng of hostlers, stable-boys, shoe-blacks, and those nameless hangers-on that infest inns and taverns and run errands, and do all kind of odd jobs for the privilege of battening on the drippings of the kitchen and the leakage of the tap-room. These all look up to him as to an oracle; treasure up his cant phrases; echo his opinions about horses and other topics of jockey lore; and, above all, endeavor to imitate his air and carriage. Every ragamuffin that has a coat to his back, thrusts his hands in the pockets, rolls in his gait, talks slang, and is an embryo Coachey.

Perhaps it might be owing to the pleasing serenity that reigned in my own mind, that I fancied I saw cheerfulness in every countenance throughout the journey. A stage-coach, however, carries animation always with it, and puts the world in motion as it whirls along. The horn, sounded at the entrance of a village, produces a general bustle. Some hasten forth to meet friends; some with bundles and band-boxes to secure places, and in the hurry of the moment can hardly take leave of the group that accompanies them. In the meantime, the coachman has a world of small commissions to execute. Sometimes he delivers a hare or pheasant; sometimes jerks a small parcel or newspaper to the door of a public house; and sometimes, with knowing leer and words of sly import, hands to some half-blushing, half-laughing housemaid an odd-shaped billet-doux from some rustic admirer. As the coach rattles through the village, everyone runs to the window, and you have glances on every side of fresh country faces and blooming, giggling girls. At the corners are assembled juntos of village idlers and wise men, who take their stations there for the important purpose of seeing company pass; but the sagest knot is generally at the blacksmith's, to whom the passing of the coach is an event fruitful of much speculation. The smith, with the horse's heel in his lap, pauses as the vehicle whirls by; the cyclops[3] round the anvil suspend their ringing hammers, and suffer the iron to grow cool; and the sooty specter in brown paper cap, laboring at the bellows, leans on the handle for a moment, and

---

3   The word has the same form in the singular and the plural. The Cyclops, a mythical race of giants with but one eye, in the middle of the forehead, were said to assist Vulcan in his workshops under Mount Etna.

permits the asthmatic engine to heave a long-drawn sigh, while he glares through the murky smoke and sulfurous gleams of the smithy.

Perhaps the impending holiday might have given a more than usual animation to the country, for it seems to me as if everybody was in good looks and good spirits. Game, poetry, and other luxuries of the table were in brisk circulation in the villages; the grocers', butchers', and fruiterers' shops were thronged with customers. The housewives were stirring briskly about, putting their dwellings in order; and the glossy branches of holly, with their bright red berries, began to appear at the windows. The scene brought to mind an old writer's account of Christmas preparations: "Now capons and hens, besides turkeys, geese, and ducks, with beef and mutton — must all die — for in twelve days[4] a multitude of people will not be fed with a little. Now plums and spice, sugar and honey, square it among pies and broth. Now or never must music be in tune, for the youth must dance and sing to get them a heat, while the aged sit by the fire. The country maid leaves half her market, and must be sent again, if she forgets a pack of cards on Christmas Eve. Great is the contention of holly and ivy, whether master or dame wears the breeches. Dice and cards benefit the butler; and if the cook do not lack wit, he will sweetly lick his fingers."

I was roused from this fit of luxurious meditation by a shout from my little traveling companions. They had been looking out of the coach windows for the last few miles, recognizing every tree and cottage as they approached home, and now there was a general burst of joy. "There's John! And there's old Carlo! And there's Bantam!" cried the happy little rogues, clapping their hands.

At the end of a lane there was an old, sober-looking servant in livery, waiting for them; he was accompanied by a superannuated pointer, and by the redoubtable Bantam, a little old rat of a pony, with a shaggy mane and long rusty tail, who stood dozing quietly by the road-side, little dreaming of the bustling times that awaited him.

---

4 Christmas festivities in the past were usually celebrated with great spirit for twelve days, or until Twelfth Night (January 6), and sometimes lasted until Candlemas (February 2).

I was pleased to see the fondness with which the little fellows leaped about the steady old footman, and hugged the pointer, who whittled his whole body for joy. But Bantam was the great object of interest; all wanted to mount at once, and it was with some difficulty that John arranged that they should ride by turns, and the eldest should ride first.

Off they set at last; one on the pony, with the dog bounding and barking before him, and the others holding John's hands; both talking at once, and overpowering him with questions about home and with school anecdotes. I looked after them with a feeling in which I do not know whether pleasure or melancholy predominated; for I was reminded of those days when, like them, I had neither known care nor sorrow, and a holiday was the summit of earthly felicity. We stopped a few moments afterwards, to water the horses; and on resuming our route, a turn of the road brought us in sight of a neat country seat. I could just distinguish the forms of a lady and two young girls in the portico, and I saw my little comrades, with Bantam, Carlo, and old John, trooping along the carriage road. I leaned out of the coach window, in hopes of witnessing the happy meeting, but a grove of trees shut it from my sight.

In the evening we reached a village where I had determined to pass the night. As we drove into the great gateway of the inn, I saw on one side the light of a rousing kitchen fire beaming through a window. I entered, and admired, for the hundredth time, that picture of convenience, neatness, and brand honest enjoyment, the kitchen of an English inn. It was of spacious dimensions, hung round with copper and tin vessels highly polished, and decorated here and there with a Christmas green. Hams, tongues, and flitches of bacon were suspended from the ceiling; a smoke-jack[5] made its ceaseless clanking beside the fireplace, and a clock ticked in one corner. A well-scoured deal table extended along one side of the kitchen, with a cold round

---

5   A kind of circular wheel or fan, horizontally placed, that was made to revolve by the upward current in the chimney. It turned a spit.

of beef, and other hearty viands, upon it, over which two foaming tankards of ale seemed mounting guard. Travelers of inferior order were preparing to attack this stout repast, whilst others sat smoking and gossiping over their ale on two high-backed oaken settles beside the fire. Trim housemaids were hurrying backwards and forwards, under the directions of a fresh, bustling landlady; but still seizing an occasional moment to exchange a flippant word, and have a rallying laugh, with the group round the fire. The scene completely realized Poor Robin's[6] humble idea of the comforts of mid-winter:

> Now trees their leafy hats do bare
> To reverence Winter's silver hair;
> A handsome hostess, merry host,
> A pot of ale now and a toast,
> Tobacco and a good coal fire,
> Are things this season doth require.

I had not been long at the inn when a post-chaise drove up to the door. A young gentleman stepped out, and by the light of the lamps I caught a glimpse of a countenance which I thought I knew. I moved forward to get a nearer view, when his eye caught mine. I was not mistaken; it was Frank Bracebridge, a sprightly, good-humored young fellow, with whom I had once traveled on the continent. Our meeting was extremely cordial, for the countenance of an old fellow traveler always brings up the recollection of a thousand pleasant scenes, odd adventures, and excellent jokes. To discuss all these in a transient interview at an inn was impossible; and finding that I was not pressed for time, and was merely making a tour of observation, he insisted that I should give him a day or two at his father's country seat, to which he was going to pass the holidays, and which lay at a few miles' distance. "It is better than eating a solitary Christmas dinner at an inn," said he, "and I can assure you of a hearty welcome, in something of the old-fashioned style." His reasoning was cogent,

---

6   Porr Robin was a pseudonym of the poet, Robert Herrick, under which he issued a series of almanacs that was begun in 1661. The passage quoted is from the number for 1694.

and I must confess the preparation I had seen for universal festivity and social enjoyment had made me feel a little impatient of my loneliness. I closed, therefore, at once, with his invitation; the chaise drove up to the door, and in a few moments I was on my way to the family mansion of the Bracebridges.

Christmas Day.

BY WASHINGTON IRVING

*From 'The Voyage
and Other English Essays,' 1820*

Dark and dull night, fly hence away,
And give the honor to this day
That sees December turned to May.
....
Why does the chilling winter's morn
Smile like a field beset with corn?
Or smell like to a Meade new-shorn,
Thus on the sudden? Come and see
The cause why things thus fragrant be.

HERRICK.

When I woke the next morning,[1] it seemed as if all the events of the preceding evening had been a dream, and nothing but the identity of the ancient chamber convinced me of their reality. While I lay musing on my pillow, I heard the sound of little feet pattering outside of the door, and a whispering consultation. Presently a choir of small voices chanted forth an old Christmas carol, the burden of which was —

---

1   Geoffrey Crayon, Gentleman, spent his Christmas Eve at Bracebridge Hall. The account which he gives of the festivities on that occasion is omitted from this book.

CHRISTMAS DAY

Rejoice, our Savior he was born
On Christmas Day in the morning.

I rose softly, slipt on my clothes, opened the door suddenly, and beheld one of the most beautiful little fairy groups that a painter could imagine. It consisted of a boy and two girls, the eldest not more than six, and lovely as seraphs. They were going the rounds of the house, and singing at every chamber door, but my sudden appearance frightened them into mute bashfulness. They remained for a moment playing on their lips with their fingers, and now and then stealing a shy glance from under their eyebrows, until, as if by one impulse, they scampered away, and as they turned an angle of the gallery, I heard them laughing in triumph at their escape.

Everything conspired to produce kind and happy feelings, in this stronghold of old-fashioned hospitality. The window of my chamber looked out upon what in summer would have been a beautiful landscape. There was a sloping lawn, a fine stream winding at the foot of it, and a tract of park beyond, with noble clumps of trees, and herds of deer. At a distance was a neat hamlet, with the smoke from the cottage chimneys hanging over it; and a church, with its dark spire in strong relief against the clear cold sky. The house was surrounded with evergreens, according to the English custom, which would have given almost an appearance of summer; but the morning was extremely frosty; the light vapor of the preceding evening had been precipitated by the cold, and covered all the trees and every blade of grass with its fine crystallizations. The rays of a bright morning sun had a dazzling effect among the glittering foliage. A robin, perched upon the top of a mountain ash that hung its clusters of red berries just before my window, was basking himself in the sunshine, and piping a few querulous notes; and a peacock was displaying all the glories of his train, and strutting with the pride and gravity of a Spanish grandee, on the terrace walk below.

I had scarcely dressed myself, when a servant appeared to invite me to family prayers. He showed me the way to a small chapel in the old wing of the house, where I found the principal part of the family already assembled in a kind of gallery, furnished with cushions, hassocks, and large prayer-books; the servants were seated on benches below. The old gentleman read prayers from a desk in front of the gallery, and Master Simon acted as clerk and made the responses; and I must do him the justice to say, that he acquitted himself with great gravity and decorum.

The service was followed by a Christmas carol, which Mr. Bracebridge himself had constructed from a poem of his favorite author, Herrick; and it had been adapted to an old church melody by Master Simon. As there were several good voices among the household, the effect was extremely pleasing; but I was particularly gratified by the exaltation of heart, and sudden sally of grateful feeling, with which the worthy squire delivered one stanza; his eye glistening, and his voice rambling out of all the bounds of time and tune:

> "'Tis thou that crown'st my glittering hearth
> > With guiltlesse mirth,
> And gives me wassaile[2] bowles to drink,
> > Spiced to the brink.
>
> Lord 'tis thy plenty-dropping hand
> > That soiles my land,
> And giv'st me, for my bushell sowne,
> > Twice ten for one."

I afterwards understood that early morning service was read on every Sunday and saint's day throughout the year, either by Mr. Bracebridge or by some member of the family. It was once almost universally the case at the seats of the nobility and gentry of England, and it is much to be regretted that the custom is falling into neglect; for the dullest observer must be sensible of the order and serenity prevalent in those households where the occasional exercise of a

---

2 From the Anglo-Saoxn, meaning *Be in health*. Hence it means the liquor with which one's health is drunk, — a kind of ale or wine flavored with nutmeg, sugar, toast, ginger, roasted apples, etc., and much used at Christmas and other festivities.

beautiful form of worship in the morning gives, as it were, the keynote to every temper for the day, and attunes every spirit to harmony.

Our breakfast consisted of what the squire denominated true old English fare. He indulged in some bitter lamentations over modern breakfasts of tea and toast, which he censured as among the causes of modern effeminacy and weak nerves, and the decline of old English heartiness; and though he admitted them to his table to suit the palates of his guests, yet there was a brave display of cold meats, wine, and ale, on the sideboard.

After breakfast, I walked about the grounds with Frank Bracebridge and Master Simon, or Mr. Simon, as he was called by everybody but the squire. We were escorted by a number of gentlemanlike dogs, that seemed loungers about the establishment; from the frisking spaniel to the steady old stag-hound — the last of which was of a race that had bee in the family time out of mind — they were all obedient to a dog-whistle which hung to Master Simon's buttonhole, and in the midst of their gambols would glance an eye occasionally upon a small switch he carried in his hand.

The old mansion had a still more venerable look in the yellow sunshine than by pale moonlight; and I could not but feel the force of the squire's idea, that the formal terraces, heavily moulded balustrades, and clipped yew trees, carried with them an air of proud aristocracy.

There appeared to be an unusual number of peacocks about the place, and I was making some remarks upon what I termed a flock of them, that were basking under a sunny wall, when I was gently corrected in my phraseology by Master Simon, who told me that, according to the most ancient and approved treatise on hunting, I must say a *muster* of peacocks. "In this same way," added he, with a slight air of pedantry, "we say a flight of doves or swallows, a bevy of quails, a herd of deer, of wrens, or cranes, a skulk of foxes, or a building of rooks." He went on to inform me that, according to Sir Anthony Fitzherbert, we ought to ascribe to this bird "both understanding and glory; for, being praised, he will presently set up his tail, chiefly against the sun, to the intent you may the better behold the beauty thereof. But at the fall of the leaf, when his tail falleth, he will mourn and hide himself in corners, till his tail come again as it was."

I could not help smiling at this display of small erudition on so whimsical a subject; but I found that the peacocks were birds of some consequence at the hall; for Frank Bracebridge informed me that they were great favorites with his father, who was extremely careful to keep up the breed, partly because they belonged to chivalry, and were in great request at the stately banquet of the olden time; and partly because they had a pomp and magnificence about them, highly becoming an old family mansion. Nothing, he was accustomed to say, had an air of greater state and dignity than a peacock perched upon an antique stone balustrade.

Master Simon had now to hurry off, having an appointment at the parish church with the village choristers, who were to perform some music of his selection. There was something extremely agreeable in the cheerful flow of animal spirits of the little man; and I confess I had been somewhat surprised at his apt quotations from authors who certainly were not in the range of everyday reading. I mentioned this last circumstance to Frank Bracebridge, who told me with a smile that Master Simon's whole stock of eradication was confined to some half a dozen old authors, which the squire had put into his hands, and which he read over and over, whenever he had a studious fit; as he sometimes had on a rainy day, or a long winter evening. Sir Anthony Fitzherbert's Book of Husbandry; Markham's Country Contentments; the Tretyse of Hunting, by Sir Thomas Cockayne, Knight; Izaak Walton's Angler, and two or three more such ancient worthies of the pen, were his standard authorities; and, like all men who know but a few books, he looked up to them with a kind of idolatry, and quoted them on all occasions. As to his songs, they were chiefly picked out of old books in the squire's library, and adapted to tunes that were popular among the choice spirits of the last century. His practical application of scraps of literature, however, had caused him to be looked upon as a prodigy of book-knowledge by all the grooms, huntsmen, and small sportsmen of the neighborhood.

While we were talking, we heard the distant toll of the village bell, and I was told that the squire was a little particular in having his household at church on a Christmas morning; considering it a day of pouring out of thanks and rejoicing; for, as old Tusser observed, —

> "At Christmas be merry, *and thankful withal,*
> And feast thy poor neighbors, the great with the
> small."

"If you are disposed to go to church," said Frank Bracebridge, "I can promise you a specimen of my cousin Simon's musical achievements. As the church is destitute of an organ, he has formed a band from the village amateurs, and established a musical club for their improvement; he has also sorted a choir, as he sorted my father's pack of hounds, according to the directions of Jervaise Markham, in his Country Contentments; for the bass he has sought out all the 'deep, solemn mouths,' and for the tenor the 'loud-ringing mouths,' among the country bumpkins; and for 'sweet mouths' he has culled with curious taste among the prettiest lassies in the neighborhood; though these last, he affirms, are the most difficult to keep in tune; your pretty female singer being exceedingly wayward and capricious, and very liable to accident."

As the morning, though frosty, was remarkably fine and clear, the most of the family walked to the church, which was a very old building of gray stone, and stood near a village, about half a mile from the park gate. Adjoining it was a low snug parsonage, which seemed coeval with the church. The front of it was perfectly matted with a yew tree, that had been trained against its walls, through the dense foliage of which, apertures had been formed to admit light into the small antique lattices. As we passed this sheltered nest, the parson issued forth and preceded us.

I had expected to see a sleek well-conditioned pastor, such as is often found in a snug living in the vicinity of a rich patron's table, but I was disappointed. The parson was a little, meagre, black-looking man, with a grizzled wig that was too wide, and stood off from each ear; so that his head seemed to have shrunk away within it, like a dried filbert in its shell. He wore a rusty coat, with great skirts, and pockets that would have held the church Bible and prayer-book: and his small legs seemed still smaller, from being planted in large shoes, decorated with enormous buckles.

I was informed by Frank Bracebridge that the parson had been a chum of his father's at Oxford, and had received this living shortly after the latter had come to his estate. He was a complete black-letter hunter,[3] and would scarcely read a work printed in the Roman character. The editions of Caxton and Wynkin de Worde were his delight; and he was indefatigable in his researches after such old English writers as have fallen into oblivion from their worthlessness. In deference, perhaps, to the notions of Mr. Bracebridge, he had made diligent investigations into the festive rites and holiday customs of former times; and had been as zealous in the inquiry, as if he had been a boon companion; but it was merely with that plodding spirit with which men of adjust[4] temperament follow up any track of study, merely because it is denominated learning; indifferent to its intrinsic nature, whether it be the illustration of the wisdom, or of the ribaldry and obscenity of antiquity. He had pored over these old volumes so intensely, that they seemed to have been reflected into his countenance; which, if the face be indeed an index of the mind, might be compared to a title-page of black-letter.

On reaching the church porch, we found the parson rebuking the gray-headed sexton for having used mistletoe among the greens with which the church was decorated. It was, he observed, an unholy plant, profane by having been used by the Druids in their mystic ceremonies; and though it might be innocently employed in the festive

---

3   That is, a person fond of collecting those earliest of English works that were printed in black-letter. Such works belong to the fourteenth century.

4   From the Latin Adustus, *inflamed* or *scorched*. It is used here in the decaying sense of *gloomy* or *melancholic*.

ornamenting of halls and kitchens, yet it had been deemed by the Fathers of the Church as unhallowed, and totally unfit for sacred purposes. So tenacious was he on this point, that the poor sexton was obliged to strip down a great part of the humble trophies of his taste, before the parson would consent to enter upon the service of the day.

The interior of the church was venerable, but simple; on the walls were several mural monuments of the Bracebridge, and just beside the altar was a tomb of ancient workmanship, on which lay the effigy of a warrior in armor, with his legs crossed, a sign of his having been a crusader. I was told it was one of the family who had signalized himself in the Holy Land, and the same whose picture hung over the fireplace in the hall.

During service, Master Simon stood up in the pew, and repeated the responses very audibly; evincing that kind of ceremonious devotion punctually observed by a gentleman of the old school, and a man of old family connections. I observed, too, that he turned over the leaves of a folio prayer-book with something of a flourish, possibly to show off an enormous seal-ring which enriched one of his fingers, and which had the look of a family relic. But he was evidently mot solicitous about the musical part of the service, keeping his eye fixed intently on the choir, and beating time with much gesticulation and emphasis.

The orchestra was in a small gallery, and presented a most whimsical grouping of heads, piled one above the other, among which I particularly noticed that of the village tailor, a pale fellow with a retreating forehead and chin, who played on the clarinet, and seemed to have blown his face to a point; and there was another, a short pursy man, stopping and laboring at a bass-viol, so as to show nothing but the top of a round bald head, like the egg of an ostrich. There were two or three pretty faces among the female singers, to which the keen air of a frosty morning had given a bright rosy tint; but the gentleman choristers had evidently been chosen, like old Cremona fiddles, more for tone than looks; and as several had to sing from the same book, there were clusterings of odd physiognomies, not unlike those groups of cherubs we sometimes see on country tombstones.

The usual services of the choir were managed tolerably well, the vocal parts generally lagging a little behind the instrumental, and some loitering fiddler now and then making up for lost time by traveling over a passage with prodigious celerity, and clearing more bars than the keenest fox-hunter to be in at the death. But the great trial was an anthem that had been prepared and arranged by Master Simon, and on which he had founded great expectation. Unluckily there was a blunder at the very outset; the musicians became flurried; Master Simon was in a fever; everything went on lamely and irregularly until they came to a chorus beginning, "Now let us sing with one accord," which seemed to be a signal for parting company: all became discord and confusion; each shifted for himself, and got to the end as well, or, rather, as soon as he could, excepting one old chorister in a pair of horn spectacles, bestriding and pinching a long, sonorous nose, who happened to stand a little apart, and, being wrapped up in his own melody, kept on a quavering course, wriggling his head, ogling his book, and winding all up by a nasal solo of at least three bars' duration.

The parson gave us a most erudite sermon on the rites and ceremonies of Christmas, and the propriety of observing it, not merely as a day of thanksgiving, but of rejoicing; supporting the correctness of his opinions by the earliest usages of the church, and enforcing them by the authorities of Theophilus of Caesarea, St. Cyprian, St. Chrysostom, St. Augustine, and a cloud more of Saints and Fathers, from whom he made copious quotations. I was a little at a loss to perceive the necessity of such a mighty array of forces to maintain a point which no one present seemed inclined to dispute; but I soon found that the good man had a legion of ideal adversaries to contend with; having, in the course of his researches on the subject of Christmas, got completely embroiled in the sectarian controversies of the Revolution, when the Puritans made such a fierce assault upon the ceremonies of the church, and poor old Christmas was driven out of the land by proclamation of Parliament.[5] The worthy parson lived but with times past, and knew but little of the present.

Shut up among worm-eaten tomes in the retirement of his antiquated little study, the pages of old times were to him as the gazettes of the day; while the ear of the Revolution was mere modern history. He forgot that nearly two centuries had elapsed since the fiery persecution of poor mince-pie throughout the land; when plum porridge was denounced as "mere popery," and roast beef as anti-Christian; and that Christmas has been brought in again triumphantly with the merry court of King Charles at the Restoration. He kindled into warmth with the ardor of his contest, and the host of imaginary foes with whom he had to combat; he had a stubborn conflict with old Prynne and two or three other forgotten champions of the Round Heads,[6] on the subject of Christmas festivity; and concluded by urging his hearers, in the most solemn and affecting manner, to stand to the traditional customs of their fathers, and feast and make merry on this joyful anniversary of the church.

I have seldom known a sermon attended apparently with more immediate effects; for on leaving the church, the congregation seemed one and all possessed with the laity of spirit so earnestly enjoined by their pastor. The elder folks gathered in knots in the churchyard, greeting and shaking hands; and the children ran about crying "Ule!

---

5   From the Flying Eagle, a small gazette, published December 24, 1652: "The House spent much time this day about the business of the navy, for settling the affairs at sea, and, before they rose, were presented with a terrible remonstrance against Christmas day, grounded upon divine Scriptures, 2 Cor. 5:16; 1 Cor. 15:14, 17; and in honor of the Lord's Day, grounded upon these Scriptures, John 20:1; Rev. 1:10; Psalm 118:24; Lev. 23:7, 11; Mark 15:8; Psalm 134:10; in which Christmas is called Anti-christ's masse, and those Masse-mongers and Papists who observe it, etc. In consequence of which Parliament spent some time in consultation about the abolition of Christmas day, passed orders to that effect, and resolved to sit on the following day, which was commonly called Christmas day." — W.I.
6   A nickname given to the Puritans, or Parliamentary party, in the reign of Charles I., in allusion to their short-cut hair. The Cavaliers, or Royalists, wore their hair in long ringlets.

Ule!" and repeating some uncouth rhymes,[7] which the parson, who had joined us, informed me had been handed down from days of yore. The villagers doffed their hats to the squire as he passed, giving him the good wishes of the season with every appearance of heartfelt sincerity, and were invited by him to the hall, to take something to keep out the cold of the weather; and I hard blessings uttered by several of the poor, which convinced me that, in the midst of his enjoyments, the worthy old cavalier had not forgotten the true Christmas virtue of charity.

On our way homeward, his heart seemed overflowed with generous and happy feelings. As we passed over a rising ground which commanded something of a prospect, the sounds of rustic merriment now and then reached our ears; the squire passed for a few moments, and looked around with an air of inexpressible benignity. The beauty of the day was, of itself, sufficient to inspire philanthropy. Notwithstanding the frostiness of the morning, the sun in his cloudless journey had acquired sufficient power to melt away the thin covering of snow from every southern declivity, and to bring out the living green which adorns an English landscape even in mid-winter. Large tracts of smiling verdure contrasted with the dazzling whiteness of the shaded slopes and hollows. Every sheltered bank, on which the broad rays rested, yielded its silver rill of cold and limpid water, glittering through the dripping grass; and sent up slight exhalations to contribute to the thin haze that hung just above the surface of the earth. There was something truly cheering in this triumph of warmth and verdure over the frosty thralldom of winter; it was, as the squire observed, an emblem of Christmas hospitality, breaking through the chills of ceremony and selfishness, and thawing every

---

7   "Ule! Ule!
         Three puddings in a pule;
         Crack nuts and cry 'Ule.'"
Ule is perhaps the same as Yule, a word that means Christmas. "Three puddings in a pule," that is, in a splutter or stew.

heart into a flow. He pointed with pleasure to the indications of good cheer reeking from the chimneys of the comfortable farmhouses and low thatched cottages. "I Loe," said he, "to see this day well kept by rich and poor; it is a great thing to have one day in the year, at least, when you are sure of being welcome wherever you go, and of having, as it were, the world all thrown open to you; and I am almost disposed to join with Poor Robin, in his malediction on every churlish enemy to this honest festival: —

"'This who at Christmas do repine,
    And would fain hence despatch him,
May they with old Duke Humphry[8] dine,
    Or else may Squire Ketch[9] catch 'em.'"

The squire went on to lament the deplorable decay of the games and amusements which were once prevalent at this season among the lower orders, and countenanced by the higher; when the old halls of castles and manor-houses were thrown open at daylight; when the tables were covered with brawn, and beef, and humming ale; when the harp and the carol resounded all day long, and when rich and poor were alike welcome to enter and make merry.[10] "Our old games

---

8   "It is cruel and shameful that the name of the worthy Duke Humphrey of Gloucester should be associated with the want of a dinner, for he was celebrated for his hospitality." *Notes and Queries.* Humphrey Plantagenet, Duke of Gloucester, was the youngest son of Henry IV, who reigned from 1399 to 1413. To dine with Duke Humphrey meant originally to have a good dinner, then to eat by the bounty of another, and finally, after the duke's death, it came to signify among his former almsmen, by a kind of irony, to go without a dinner. Another account plausibly attributes the proverb to a wit who came down from London with a party of friends to dine at the White Hart Inn at St. Albans, but who was accidentally shut up in the Abbey of St. Albans, where Humphrey lay buried, and so lost his dinner.

9   Also known as Jack Ketch, a name given in England to the public hangman or executioner.

10   An English gentleman at the opening of the great day, i.e. on Christmas day in the morning, had all his tenants and neighbors enter his hall by daybreak. The strong beer was broached, and the black jacks went plentifully about with toast, sugar and nutmeg, and good Cheshire cheese. The Hackin (the great sausage) must be boiled by daybreak, or else two young men must take the maiden (i.e. the cook) by the arms and run her round

36

and local customs," said he, "had a great effect in making the peasant fond of his home, and the promotion of them by the gentry made him fond of his lord. They made the times merrier, and kinder, and better, and I can truly say, with one of our old poets, —

"'I like them well—the curious preciseness
And all-pretended gravity of those
That seek to banish hence these harmless sports,
Have thrust away much ancient honestly.'

"The nation," continued he, "is altered; we have almost lost our simple true-hearted peasantry. They have broken asunder from the higher classes, and seem to think their interests are separate. They have become too knowing, and begin to read newspapers, listen to alehouse politicians, and talk of reform. I think one mode to keep them in good humor in these hard times would be for the nobility and gentry to pass more time on their estates, mingle more among the country people, and set the merry old English games going again."

Such was the good squire's project for mitigating public discontent: and, indeed, he had once attempted to put his doctrine in practice, and a few years before had kept open house during the holidays in the old style. The country people, however, did not understand how to play their parts in the scene of hospitality; many uncouth circumstances occurred; the manor was overrun by all the vagrants of the country, and more beggars drawn into the neighborhood in one week than the parish officers could get rid of in a year. Since then, he had contented himself with inviting the decent part of the neighboring peasantry to call at the hall on Christmas Day, and with distributing beef, and bread, and ale, among the poor, that they might make merry in their own dwellings.

We had not been long home when the sound of music was heard from a distance. A band of country lads, without coats, their shirt sleeves fancifully tied with ribbons, their hats decorated with greens,

---

the marketplace till she is shamed of her laziness." (Quoted by Irving from 'Round about our Sea-Coal Fire.')

and club sin their hands, were seen advancing up the avenue, followed by a large number of villagers and peasantry. They stopped before the hall door, where the music struck up a peculiar air, and the lads performed a curious and intricate dance, advancing, retreating, and striking their clubs together, keeping exact time to the music; while one, whimsically crowned with a fox's skin, the tail of which flaunted down his back, kept capering round the skirts of the dance, and rattling a Christmas-box with many antic gesticulations.

The squire eyed this fanciful exhibition with great interest and delight, and gave me a full account of its origin, which he traced to the times when the Romans held possession of the island; plainly proving that this was a lineal descendant of the sword-dance of the ancients. "It was now," he said, "nearly extinct, but he had accidentally met with traces of it in the neighborhood, and had encouraged its revival; though, to tell the truth, it was too apt to be followed up by the rough cudgel-play, and broken heads in the evening."

After the dance was concluded, the whole party was entertained with brawn and beef, and stout home-brewed. The squire himself mingled among the rustics, and was received with awkward demonstrations of deference and regard. It is true, I perceived two or three of the younger peasants, as they were raising their tankards to their mouths, when the squire's back was turned, making something of a grimace, and giving each other the wink; but the moment they caught my eye they pulled grave faces, and were exceedingly demure. With Master Simon, however, they all seemed more at their ease. His varied occupations and amusements had made him well known throughout the neighborhood. He was a visitor at every farmhouse and cottage; gossiped with the farmers and their wives; romped with their daughters; and, like that type of a vagrant bachelor, the humble-be, tolled the sweets from all the rosy lips of the country round.

The bashfulness of the guests soon gave way before good cheer and affability. There is something genuine and affectionate in the gaiety of the lower orders, when it is excited by the bounty and familiarity of those above them; the warm glow of gratitude enters into their mirth, and a kind word or a small pleasantry frankly uttered by a patron, gladdens the heart of the dependent more than oil and wine. When the squire had retired, the merriment increased, and there was much joking and laughter, particularly between Master Simon and a hale, ruddy-faced, white-headed farmer, who appeared to be the wit of the village; for I observed all his companions to wait with open mouths for his retorts, and burst into a gratuitous laugh before they could well understand them.

The whole house indeed seemed abandoned to merriment; as I passed to my room to dress for dinner, I heard the sound of music in a small court, and looking through a window that commanded it, I perceived a band of wandering musicians, with panda pipes and tambourine; a pretty, coquettish housemaid was dancing a jig with a smart country lad, while several of the other servants were looking on. In the midst of her sport the girl caught a glimpse of my face at the window, and, coloring up, ran off with an air of roguish affected confusion.

The Story of a Christmas Story.

BY HENRY LITCHFIELD WEST

From 'The Bookman' magazine, 1919

THIS IS a story of a Christmas story. It is inspired by the hope that it may induce the goodly company of THE BOOKMAN fellowship to join with me on Christmas morning in reading "A Christmas Carol" by Charles Dickens. For many, many years, in the early hours of Christmas day, I have taken "A Christmas Carol" from its place upon the bookshelf and read it through from beginning to end — from the first line, "Marley was dead to begin with," to the last words, "God bless us, every one." And when I reach the page where Scrooge, awaking in the morning after his nocturnal wanderings with his ghostly companions, puts his head out of the window and asks a small boy if he knows what day it is, and the boy explodes with the answer, "It is CHRISTMAS DAY!" (always in small capitals), my pulse throbs faster, my heart beats more rapidly, and my eyes weep tears of delirious joy. I would not miss that thrill on Christmas morning for many, many dollars! There is no better way of putting one's soul in complete harmony with the joyous, generous festival. It is impossible to read the story without experiencing a thorough warming of the cockles of the heart. It makes one wish for Aladdin's lamp, so as to command a fortune large enough to carry Christmas into every home. Thackeray had this feeling, for in writing of the "Carol" he said it would unquestionably lead to the purchase of everything in all the shops!

When I read the story for the twentieth time on last Christmas morning, — the seventy-fifth anniversary of its first publication, — I realized that I knew nothing of its background. Instantly a score of questions framed themselves in my mind. When and where did Dickens write the story? What was its inspiration? Was there a real Scrooge, or Bob Cratchit, or Tiny Tim? Was the "Carol" appreciated by others as it was loved by me? Forthwith I began a quest which, for nearly a year, has been a delightful recreation. It has led me into many libraries and a multitude of old bookstores; it has resulted in a delightful long-distance acquaintance with congenial book collectors; and, through correspondence, it has carried me into the sacred precincts of the British Museum. Perhaps there are others who, like me, having been thrilled by the conversion of Scrooge, softened by the tenderness of Tiny Tim, and cheered by the heartiness of Scrooge's nephew, will be glad to read the story again in the light of its environment. Some of these days, I hope to make my quest complete. I have never seen the original manuscript, nor even a first edition; nor have I been able to learn whether the characters were purely imaginary or drawn from life. There are many things yet to be done which are fully worthwhile, not the least being a monograph which will present, in far more detail than is permissible within the limits of this article, the story of the "Carol" from every angle.

Charles Dickens wrote many Christmas stories. All of them came from his heart. The season of gladness and cheer appealed to his emotional and sentimental nature. He was saturated with the Yuletide spirit; and these Christmas tales literally gushed forth from the well-springs of his soul. "My Purpose," he says, in an introduction to one of the editions of the Christmas stories, "was, in a whimsical kind of mask which the good humor of the season justified, to awaken some loving and forbearing thoughts never out of season in a Christian land." We may well inquire, as Gilbert K. Chesterton has done, how it happened "that this bustling, nineteenth-century man, full of the almost cock-sure common sense of the utilitarian and liberal epoch, came to associate his name chiefly in literary history with the perpetuation of a half-pagan and half-Catholic festival." Mr. Chesterton's answer to the question is characteristic of his keen analytical mind. He specifies three qualities which explain the hold of Christmas upon the human sense of happiness — the dramatic quality, the contrast of indoor feasting and revelry with the discomforts of exterior wintry weather, and the element of the grotesque. "If we study," he says, "the real atmosphere of rejoicing and of riotous charity in 'The Christmas Carol,' we shall find that all the three marks I have mentioned are unmistakably visible." The "Carol" is a happy story, he says, because it describes an abrupt and dramatic change. "It is not only the story of a conversion but of a sudden conversion." It is a tale of winter, with its comfort saved from enervation by a tingle of something bitter and bracing in the weather. "Lastly," says Chesterton, "the story exemplifies throughout the power of the third principle — the kinship between gaiety and the picturesque. Everybody is happy because nobody is dignified."

Dickens was thirty-one years old when, in the early part of October 1843, he visited Manchester. It was during this tour that the idea of the "Carol" entered his mind. His fame had already been established by "Pickwick Papers," "Oliver Twist," "Nicholas Nickleby," and "The Old Curiosity Shop," and he was at work upon "Martin Chuzzlewit." He began the "Carol" while at Manchester, finishing it upon his return to 1 Devonshire Terrace, and completing the task in five or six weeks. The work was done under high pressure. He wrote to Sir Edward Bulwer-Lytton that while he was writing the story he was so closely occupied with it "that I never left home before the owls went out, and led quite a solitary life." The tale completely obsessed him. He wrote to Professor Felton on January 2, 1844:

Over which Christmas Carol Charles Dickens wept, and laughed, and wept again, and excited himself in the most extraordinary manner in the composition, and thinking whereof he walked about the black streets of London, fifteen and twenty miles, many a night when all the sober folks had gone to bed. .... To keep the Chuzzlewit going, and to do this little book the "Carol" in the odd times between parts of it, was, as you may suppose, pretty tight work. But when it was done I broke out like a madman.

Published shortly before Christmas, 1843, by Chapman and Hall, on commission for the author, in one volume of foolscap octavo, one hundred and sixty-six pages, and containing four colored illustrations and four woodcuts by John Leech, the story was described on the title page as "A Christmas Carol, in prose, being a ghost story of Christmas." The preface, dated December 1843, was as follows:

> "I have endeavored in this Ghostly little book, to raise the Ghost of an Idea, which shall not put my readers out of humor with themselves, with each other, with the season, or with me. May it haunt their houses pleasantly, and no one wish to lay it.
> Their Faithful Friend and Servant,
>
> C.D."

The success of the book was instantaneous. Dickens, writing to Macready, characterized it as "prodigious — the greatest, I think, I have ever achieved." All manner of strangers wrote to him by every post "about their homes and hearths, and how this same 'Carol' is read aloud there, and kept on a little shelf by itself." Lord Jeffrey sensed the psychological value of the tale when he wrote to Dickens that "you may be sure you have done more good by this little publication, fostered more kindly feelings, and prompted more positive acts of beneficence, than can be traced to all the pulpits and confessionals in Christendom since 1842." Douglas Jerrold, by whom John Leech was recommended as the illustrator of the "Carol," wrote a most appreciative notice in "Punch," and Henry Chorley rendered a like service in "The Athenaeum." It was the former review which led Dickens to write from Cremona to Jerrold that "it was very hearty and good of you, Jerrold, to make that affectionate mention of the 'Carol' in 'Punch,' and I assure you it was not lost on the distant object of your manly regard, but touched him as you wished and meant it should." The best tribute, however, came from Thackeray, who, while in Switzerland, had received a box of novels. These he reviewed in "Fraser's Magazine." "And now there is but one book left in the box," he wrote, "the smallest one, but oh, how much the best of all." His tribute to the story fairly pulsates with enthusiasm. One can imagine dear old Thackeray, his face beaming with smiles and his eyes twinkling behind his spectacles, as he wrote:

In fact, one might as well detail the plot of "The Merry Wives of Windsor" or "Robinson Crusoe," as recapitulate here the adventures of Scrooge, the miser, and his Christmas conversion. I am not sure that the allegory is a very complete one, and protest, with the classics, against the use of blank verse in prose; but here all objections stop. Who can listen to objections regarding such a book as this? It seems to me a national benefit, and to every man or woman who reads it, a personal kindness.

The last two people I heard speak of it were women; neither knew the other, or the author, and both said, by way of criticism, "God bless him!" A Scotch philosopher, who nationally does not keep Christmas, on reading the book, sent out for a turkey, and asked two friends to dine — this is a fact! Many men were known to sit down after perusing it, and write off letters to their friends, not about business, but out of their fullness of heart, and to wish old acquaintances a happy Christmas. Had the book appeared a fortnight earlier, all the prize cattle would have been gobbled up in pure love and friendship, Epping denuded of sausages, and not a turkey left in Norfolk. His royal highness's fat stock would have fetched unheard of prices, and Alderman Bannister would have been tired of slaying. But there is a Christmas for 1844, too; the book will be as early then as now, and so let the spectators look out.

As for Tiny Tim, there is a certain passage in the book regarding that young gentleman, about which a man should hardly venture to speak in print or in public, any more than he would of any other affections of his private heart. There is not a reader in England but that little creature will be a bond of union between the author and him; and he will say of Charles Dickens, as the women just now, "GOD BLESS HIM!" What a feeling is this for a writer to be able to inspire and what a reward to reap!

There was, however, a fly in the ointment. The expense of publishing the book proved to be out of all proportion to the revenue. "Want of judgment had been shown in not adjusting the expenses of production to the selling price," is the explanation offered by Mr. Forster, Dickens' biographer. In a volume dealing with the first editions of Dickens' books, written by John C. Eckel, and published by Chapman and Hall in 1913, there is more detail. Mr. Eckel writes:

Knowing that he had written something of extraordinary merit, Dickens began to plan a suitable presentation of his effort. For the first time, and, incidentally, the last, he went in for color, not only for the title page, but also for the important etchings. The result was an artistic success, but a financial disappointment to the author. The greatest Christmas book ever written in any language delighted many thousands of readers but contributed to the unhappiness of the man who wrote it. The cost of the production had been too extravagant for a five-shilling book.

The first edition of six thousand was speedily sold and the second and third editions soon followed. In February 1844, Dickens received his first statement from his publishers, and his share of the receipts seemed to be pitifully small. He wrote to Forster:

Such a night as I have passed. I really believed I should never get up again until I had passed through all the horrors of a fever. I found the "Carol" accounts awaiting me and they were the cause of it. The first six thousand copies show a profit of £230. And the last four will yield as much more. I had set my soul upon a thousand clear. What a wonderful thing it is that such a great success should occasion me such intolerable anxiety and disappointment.

Even though fifteen thousand copies had been sold by the end of 1844, netting Dickens a profit of £726, the shock of the meager return had much to do with the severance of the relations between Dickens and his publishers. Eventually a reconciliation occurred but, in the meantime, several editions of the "Carol" bear the imprint of Bradbury and Evans. This was the firm to whom Dickens turned when he squabbled with his first publishers, and he remained with his new associates until 1859. Then he had a dispute with them and the connection ceased. Ley says in "The Dickens Circle":

In the years between 1844 and 1858 there was considerable friendliness with both Bradbury and Evans. They were familiar guests at the Devonshire House; and with Evans, at any rate, there could not have been an absolute rupture of the friendship, for the novelist's eldest son had fallen in love with the publisher's daughter, and in November, 1861, Charles Dickens, the younger, was married to Miss Evans.

As originally published, the "Carol" was bound in brown cloth, with gilt edges, and with the title stamped in type of quaint, old-fashioned design, also gilded. A gilded wreath of holly leaves added to the ornamentation. Altogether, twenty-four editions were issued in the original form, the only change being the substitution of crimson for brown cloth in the binding. The title page in colors led to results which have been of great interest to book collectors. The very first issues were printed in red and blue and the heading of the first chapter appeared as "Stave 1." The book had not been on the press very long, however, before "Stave 1" was changed to "Stave One"; and Dickens experimented with red and green instead of red and blue, although later, there was a return to the latter colors. It is difficult to understand why red and blue were chosen for they make the title page look like a Fourth of July poster, while red and green are the commonly accepted Christmas colors. Another variant was in the use of end papers, green being used in some books and cream color in others. There has, consequently, been considerable confusion regarding the identity of the several editions, but "among experts," says Eckels, "it is agreed that the real first issue is the red and blue title page and the green end papers, with the error mentioned." The green and red issue with the green end papers and "Stave 1" instead of "Stave One" is by far the most costly at the present day, because of its great scarcity. A copy of this issue was sold by a London book firm in 1912 for £32.

There are quite a number of copies of the first edition in the United States. At an exhibition held in St. Louis, in February 1912, under the auspices of the Franklin Club, two were shown. One, from the collection of William K. Bixby, contains an inscription, "Mrs. Henry Austin, from Charles Dickens, Devonshire Terrace, Friday, December 22, 1843". Another copy was loaned by Frederick W. Lehmann, a distinguished lawyer of St. Louis. Still another copy was included in the Hoe Library (sold by Anderson in April 1911), but it was sold to a London dealer. In the same year, another copy, belonging to the library of A.S. Whiton, of New York, was sold by Freeman and brought $46.00. This copy bore the bookplate of Reverend George Richard Mackarness, M.A. The average price of the first issues of the first edition in red and blue is $50.00. It is quite difficult, except in the case of presentation copies, to obtain perfect volumes. Mr. Eckel explains:

"The Christmas Carol" achieved wonderful popularity at once and each little volume was eagerly read and reread many times. Crisp and unsoiled copies in the original state, as a consequence, are rather difficult of acquirement. The binding was rather frail, and the leaves became shaky and somewhat loose. These conditions forced rebinding and that explains the presence of many such copies on the market. Another habit prevailed for many years of rebinding uniformly all the Christmas books, and this again was fatal to numberless "Carols."

The Library of Congress does not contain a first edition. The earliest copy in that collection is of the tenth edition, published in 1844, bound in crimson cloth, with gilt letters, and illustrated with the colored plates drawn by Leech. The most precious copy is the one which Dickens sent to Thackeray with this autograph inscription: "W. M. Thackeray from Charles Dickens (whom he made very happy once a long way from home)." Mr. Ley says that he has been unable to trace the meaning of this allusion but adds that this copy of the "Carol" has an interesting history, for, when, after Thackeray's death, his belongings were sold by auction, Queen Victoria sent an unlimited commission to buy it, becoming its possessor for £25 10s.

We have the authority of Charles Dickens, the younger, for the statement that the "Carol" shares with "Pickwick" and "David Copperfield" the distinction of being the most universally popular of all the works of Charles Dickens. The assertion is demonstrated by the great number of reprints. The book was issued steadily by Chapman and Hall, and Bradbury and Evans, the demand being met by cheap editions at a shilling and nine pence each. The old stereotyped plates were used by Chapman and Hall in 1873 for an edition on post-octavo paper, each page surrounded with red rule to fill the larger sheet. In the Library of Congress there are thirty-eight distinct reprints and it is conceded that the collection is incomplete. The story has been translated into French, German, Danish and other languages; it has been embossed for use of the blind; it has been transcribed in many systems of stenography; and (a travesty indeed) it has been rewritten by someone who thought it was unintelligible for children. Elbert Hubbard has preserved it in a high example of the typographical art. It is found in numberless collections of the best stories in English literature and it has attracted many artists, including Maclise, Landseer, Frederick Barnard and F. O. C. Darley. None of the reprints has the distinct charm and value which attaches to the volume in which the original manuscript is reproduced. The priceless sheets of Dickens' handiwork were given by him to Mr. Mitten, his old schoolfellow and solicitor. In some way they drifted into Sotheby's auction rooms in 1875, when they were purchased by a bookseller for £55, being afterward resold to Sir Stuart M. Samuel. In 1890 they were reproduced in facsimile with an introduction by F. G. Kitton, and five hundred copies of the publication were imported into this country by Brentano. These were speedily sold and went into the libraries of collectors. The writing shows every evidence of rapid work, although there are comparatively few erasures or corrections.

The popularity of the "Carol" was, in one way, a source of great annoyance to the author. It was pirated in many directions. In one case of peculiar flagrancy he accepted the advice of Thomas Noon Talfourd and John Forster and began an action in the Court of Chancery. The case was successful, except that Dickens was unable to get any costs out of the defendant, but it gave him much vexation. "I shall not easily forget the expense and anxiety, and horrible injustice of the 'Carol' case," he wrote afterward, when there was a question whether he ought not to institute proceedings in another case, "wherein, in asserting the plainest right on earth, I was really treated as if I were the robber instead of the robbed. . . . And I know of nothing that could come, even of a successful action, which would be worth the mental trouble and disturbance it would cost." At the same time, his sense of humor did not desert him. The case was so flagrant that the Vice Chancellor would not even listen to the argument which Talfourd had carefully prepared. Dickens' sympathy was mingled with amusement. "Oh, the agony of Talfourd at Knight Bruce's not hearing him," he wrote to Forster. "He had sat up 'till three in the morning, he says, preparing his speech, and would have done all kind of things with the affidavits!" Even as late as 1869, says Charles Dickens, the younger, one of these imitations was published under the title, "Christmas Eve with the Spirits, or The Canon's Wanderings through Ways Unknown."

Another curious phase of the "Carol" is illustrated by the many attempts which have been made to dramatize it. The story in dialogue for acting is to be found in every library but these efforts may be dismissed with brief comment. They are sad failures, a fact not difficult to understand. The atmosphere of the book is in the sentences and paragraphs which cannot be transplanted to the stage. It is no wonder that Dickens was not favorably impressed when he witnessed the presentation at the Savoy and the Adelphi. He characterized the impersonation of Bob Cratchit as "heartbreaking," and exclaimed in a letter, "Oh, Heaven! If any forecast of this was ever in my mind . . ." And this brings us to the consideration of what was in Dickens' mind when he created his characters in the "Carol." Did he picture real people or did he merely imagine them? The question cannot be answered satisfactorily because all efforts to find human prototypes in actual existence have proven a failure. "Who's Who in Dickens" throws no light upon the subject, nor is there information in the large and interesting volume dealing with the originals of Dickens' characters. In none of these works is there any indication that the "squeezing, wrenching, grasping, scraping, clutching, covetous old sinner" known as Scrooge had an actual counterpart among the persons whom Dickens met in daily life. The same is true regarding all the other characters in the story.

Another interesting fact connected with "A Christmas Carol" is that Dickens used it as the medium for the first of the platform readings which afterward became so famous. When the Midland Institute was established in Birmingham in 1853, a benefit performance was given and Dickens was invited to participate. As the date was December 27, the "Carol" was the most appropriate feature, and his reading of the story marked the debut of his platform appearance. It is easy to imagine that the cordial appreciation which followed the infusion of his own personality into the characters of the "Carol" opened for him a vista of possibilities which he could not afford to ignore. He always placed the "Carol" on his program con amore, and one occasion inspired a delightful letter to Mary Boyle. "I have just been reading my 'Christmas Carol' in Yorkshire," he wrote to her. "I should have lost my heart to the beautiful young lady of the hotel (age twenty-nine, dress, black frock and jacket, exquisitely braided), if it had not been safe in your possession." At the same time he enclosed a kiss to Mary, "if you will have the kindness to return it when done with."

THE STORY OF A CHRISTMAS STORY

It is not necessary to review the "Carol" itself; I am content to accept Mr. Ley's judgment that it is Dickens' "noblest work," and to read with appreciation the commendations of Thackeray, Lord Jeffrey, Sidney Smith, Thomas Hood, Austin Dobson, Andrew Lang, G. K. Chesterton, E.P. Whipple, and a score of other eminent commentators who place the "Carol" upon the highest pinnacle of literary achievement. It has been a pleasure to me to search every nook and cranny for the stray facts which, when woven together, tell this story of a Christmas story. Some of these days, God willing, I will fill a shelf with every known edition of the "Carol," from the cheap, ten-cent "English classic" to the costly issue on vellum; but still in the place of honor will be the well-worn volume which has been my constant companion for so many years. In the meantime, I hope that what I have written may lead the readers of THE BOOKMAN to take up the "Carol" with a new delight. If, in the reading, one does not, like Dickens, weep and laugh and weep again, he cannot hope to know what Christmas really means, and can only regret that he is the sad possessor of an ossified heart.

Christmas Carols, Ancient and Modern.

BY ANNIE RUSSELL MARBLE

From 'The Bookman' magazine, December 1910

IN THE nomenclature of literature and music, few terms are more flexible, both as regards substance and form, than the word "carol." With its derivation still a mooted question, it has extended its range to include nearly all festival songs. From earliest times to the present, amid great diversity of models, there have been two generic types: First, the carol of exultation, closely linked with the primal use of the song as accompaniment to the dance, and second, the carol of adoration, more stately and restrictive, akin to the early Biblical hymns of praise. Moreover, the history of these two elemental carol forms is coeval, and often interlinked, rather than sequential. The Saturnalian feasts of the Romans, the Mother-Night, or Yule-Feast, of the Saxons, both occurring during the latter days of December, were celebrated with dance-songs of joy; the Hebrews commemorated their early victories by adoration of Jehovah, with "singing and dancing, with tabrets, with joy and with instruments of musick."

Retrospect of carol singing, however, seldom reverts beyond the early Christian centuries. The birth and mission of Christ inspired existent forms and customs with new meaning and spirit. After Clemens Romanus, about 70, decreed that the Nativity should be celebrated on December 25, a date already associated with pagan festivals, the religious songs gradually and consistently became carols of adoration to Christ and the Madonna, and from these early hymns of the Nativity were developed the varied odes of adoration suggested by the term "Christmas carol." As early as the seventh year of the second century, the younger Pliny wrote to the Emperor Trajan that Christians "gathered on festival days to sing praises alternately to God and Christ."

In the meantime, the dance-carol, the old-time karolle, became the medium of secular exultation and feasting, associated with the decorative and material elements of Christmas celebration, with the holly and bay, the ivy and mistletoe, the wassail and the *pièce de resistance* of the holiday feast, the entrance of the boar's head. Dryden aptly commingled his trio of terms:

> The costly feast, the carol, and the dance.

Thus, in the older Latin poets, in Boccaccio and Chaucer, the word "carol" has this meaning, always associated with movements of merriment.

Recognizing the popularity of rhythmic song as an element of worship, the monks wrote the Latin hymns and canticles from the famous stanzas of St. Ambrose and Prudentius in the fourth century and the Gregorian chant of the sixth century to the more undulating "Nowell" carols of medieval times, which had its model in the jubilant first song of the shepherds on the Judean plains. When Augustine was sent to England, he was directed by Gregory to retain as many of the festival customs as were consistent with the dignity of Christian religion. Accordingly, he allowed the feasts, encouraged the songs, but prohibited the demoralizing pagan dances. A favorite form of early religious carols in England was a hybrid of Latin and English, exampled in the boar's-head carol, quoted by Irving in *The Sketch Book*, or the more strictly worshipful stanzas, beginning:

> Puer nobis natus est de Maria virgine,
> Be glad, lordynges, be the more or lesse,

> I bring you tydings of gladnesse,
> As Gabriel me bereth witnesse.

During the Middle Ages there was increasing use of the carols both on the Continent and in England. In France, the Noel, or natal canticle, contains legends and expressions similar to the coeval English carol, while the pilgrimage songs in Italy and Spain have kindred themes and incentives. The masque and "Feast of Fools," with the unrestrained "Lord of Misrule," tending toward license and riotous excess, refused to yield its sway over the dramatic imaginations of the people until the substitution, by the priests and guilds, of the Mysteries, Miracle-Plays and Moralities, reaching their greatest popularity during the twelfth to fifteenth centuries. To these crude representations of mingled religious fact, tradition and fiction, full of anachronisms and absurdities, may be traced not alone the beginnings of English drama, but also the concepts and forms of many English carols, selected from their song-interludes. In the Townley mysteries was the song of the shepherds, the primal version of a later popular carol:

> That chylde is borne
> At Bethlehem this morne
> Ye shall find Him beforne
> Betwixt two bestys.

The famous lullaby carol, to be noted later, was the refrain in the Coventry mystery of the Shearmen and the Tailors of the fifteenth century.

The Miracle-Plays, acted as late as the reign of Queen Anne on special occasions, have a definite place in both the religious and secular history of England; likewise, the carols were sung in the churches and at the courts; they formed the themes of trained choristers, and they were also the songs of the wandering minstrels and royal waits. The composition of carols became a lucrative profession for bishops, poets and minstrels. In 1201, King John gave 25s to the clerks who chanted carols at his court; Henry VII gave £1 for the composition of a carol, and a similar sum was paid to the "tune-setter" and to the singers.

CHRISTMAS CAROLS

Christmas was primarily the great festival of kings, from the crowning of Charlemagne on Christmas, 800, to the coronation of William the Conqueror, in 1066, on Christmas Day. On the same festival, in 1065, Westminster Abbey was consecrated, thus linking church and state in religious pomp and ceremony. Under Henry VIII. these festivities reached their climax, excepting on the "first still Christmas" of 1525, when the severe illness of the king prohibited "carols, bells or merry-making." At this time one notes the two distinctive classes of the carols: the religious, usually sung by chorus-boys or bands of waits; and the festive carols, sung at feasts by hired minstrels or by the entire company of guests. In 1521 a collection of these convivial carols was made by Wynkyn de Worde; they include wassail songs, boar's-head carols and responses, and recitals, in rude verse, of the rival claims of holly, ivy and bay, the decorative emblems retained from the customs of ancient Romans, Goths and Druids. Among the oldest and most typical of these holly carols is the stanza:

> Holly and Ivy made a great party,
> Who should have the mastery
> In lands where they go.
> Then spake Holly, "I am friske and jolly,
> I will have the mastery
> In lands where we go."

Carol sheets were sold in London and elsewhere by street hawkers as early as the thirteenth century and as late as the eighteenth. It seems strange, as well as regretful, that so few carols have been preserved either on broad sides or in collections, since there are records of collations in 1521, 1546 and 1562. In the latter year John Tysdale was given license to print "Certayne goodly Carowles to be songe to the glory of God." In 1661 was issued the collection, to which students are greatly indebted, "The New Carols for the Merry Time of Christmas to Sundry Pleasant Tunes." On one of the early carol sheets appeared an illustration, retained in various forms in later issues, an interesting embodiment of sundry legends interwoven into earlier masques. In a rude woodcut is represented the stable at Bethlehem with a group-picture of the Holy Family, surrounded by an ox, a cow, a sheep, a raven and a cock. From the mouth of each animal extends a Latin inscription, and together these form a dialogue, thus: The cock, "Christus natus est"; the raven, "Quando?" the cow, "Hac nocte"; the ox, "Ubi, Ubi?" the sheep, "Bethlehem." In the carols and pantomimes alike the traditions of the cock were popular: The cock, roasted alive, returns to life to announce Christ's birth or the yet more familiar superstition, mentioned by Shakespeare, that the cock crows all night before Christmas, thus banishing all witches and spirits of evil. During the age of euphemism and verbal conceits, the clowns in the pantomimes delighted not alone in the myths and fancies of Christmas and Twelfth Night, but also in crude puns upon carols, as "A Christmas carol doth make old Care howl."

As was inevitable, these carols, sung by diverse bands and in many localities, had wide variations of form. A manuscript of the fifteenth century, probably the property of a professed minstrel under Henry VI, and now in the British Museum, was edited in 1847 by Mr. Thomas Wright of London; in this volume one finds the most accessible form of the best known early carols. Here is the Latin "Nowell" chant, the melodious "In Excelsis Gloria," and the lullaby carol, a dialogue between Mary and Jesus, the Babe. This is sometimes called "This Endris Night" from the opening lines:

> This endris night, ("endris" translated last.)
> I saw a sight,
> A star as bright as day;
> And ever among
> A maiden sung,
> Lullay, byby, lullay.

In sentiment, no less than cadence, this is one of the most beautiful of the early carols, as the last stanza suggests:

> Now, sweet son, since it is so, all things are at thy will,
> I pray thee grant me a boon, if it be right and skill,

That child or man,
That will and can,
Be merry upon thy day;
To bliss them bring,
And I shall sing
Lullay, byby, lullay.

The Yule Carol, with its extended welcome to saints and martyrs, old and young, is another significant song of rejoicing. Kindred in joyance and resonant rhythm is the more familiar carol:

God rest you, Merry Gentlemen,
Let nothing you dismay,
Remember Christ, our Savior,
Was born on Christmas Day;
To save us all from Satan's pow'r,
When we were gone astray;

O tidings of comfort and joy,
O tidings of comfort and joy!

Sharing the antiquity and the popularity of these earlier carols cited, is the legendary narrative of "Saint Stephen, the clerk," the "cherry tree carol," corresponding to similar accounts of Joseph's old age and his miraculous revelation of the innocence of Mary embodied in French and Dutch carols, and the repetitive merry measures of the song, "I Saw Three Ships Come Sailing By."

In this early collection of carols are a few so-called "moral-songs," somewhat prophetic of the less joyous, more morose warnings of the later Puritan hymnists. One of the most typical of such carols, entitled "Remember, O Thou Man," is found in a publication in 1611 by Thos. Ravenscroft, "Melismata, Musical Phansies, Fitting the Court, Citie and Countrie Humours, To 3, 4, and 5 Voyces, To all delightfull, except to the spitefull, to none offensive, except to the Pensive." In reiterated measures the memory is exhorted to

Remember Adam's fall, from Heaven to Hell,
Remember Adam's fall, how we were condemn'd all,
In Hell perpetual, Therefor to dwell.

Fortunately, the carol does not end with this lugubrious vision, but offers joy and happiness through repentance and Christ's redemption.

As the Puritan element came into power the natural reaction was shown upon all festive songs and emblems of Christmastide. Street heralds with hoarse bells, proclaiming, 'No Christmas!" took the place of the carols of rejoicing and good cheer. The Puritan clergy, however, did not abolish the use of the carol music, but gave it a strange transformation in adaptations to their solemn psalms. Shakespeare in "The Winter's Tale" describes his one Puritan as singing "psalms to hornpipes." In 1630 was printed by Robert Yong and collated by William Slayter "Certaine of David's Psalmes intended for Christmas Carols, fitted to the most sollemne times, everywhere familiarlie used." In a later reprint, 1642, of this collection, in the British Museum, are marginal comments, suggesting the adaptations to ballad and carol tunes, thus: Psalm 6 to "Jane Shore," Psalm 9 to "Bara Forster's Dream," Psalm 43 to "Crimson Velvet," and Psalm 47 to "Garden Greene." As example of the extreme gloom of these Puritan hymns, one recalls the familiar exhortation of Thomas Delomey to "All Ye that are to mirth inclined."

The Restoration brought revival, in extreme fashion, of all forbidden festival rites, and during the later seventeenth century the more riotous carols exceeded the popularity of the religious and commemorative odes. After a few years of excessive revelry in the keeping of Christmas, interest in the earlier, abused festivities waned. "Poor Robin's Almanack," which had been the storehouse of many a wassail-song and carol of blithe spirit, in 1702 lamented the decadence of jollity and feasting:

But now landlords and tenants, too,
In making feasts are very slow;
*****

Yet some true English blood still lives,
Who gifts to the poor at Christmas gives.

There are not a few parallelisms between the history of the English drama and English carols; their interdependence has been noted; they both suffered submergence during the Protectorate and after a few years of spasmodic and sporadic revival, they both lost their popularity as spectacular festivities and became more allied with literature and less with popular presentation. As the larger portion of the English dramas by the poets of the literary power during the last two centuries have been written to be read rather than to be acted, so the carols of this same period have been more familiar to the student of literature than to the searcher for songs. In parts of rural England and in some Continental districts, carol singing on the streets at Christmas-tide is still a charming reminder, but its widespread picturesqueness as a custom has wholly disappeared. In the churches, however, carols still form a prominent part of the Christmas service, and the recent attempt to revive carol singing on the steps of church and chapel is a laudable return to an effective and impressive celebration.

The carols sung today, like those of former centuries, vary much in literary and musical value. Many of those in use in Sunday Schools are vapid and inferior to their earlier models. Among the oldest carols, whose melody is heard often, is the familiar exhortation accredited to J. Reading in 1692:

Come, all ye faithful,
Joyful and triumphant.

In 1703, Nahum Tate wrote the pictorial carol, "While Shepherds Watched Their Flocks by Night," and the old melody, no less than the narrative, finds favor at each Christmastide. There is a perennial triumph in the natal-song:

Joy to the world, the Lord is come,
Let earth receive her King,

Whose melody by Handel and words by Watts date back to the early eighteenth century. With yet more exultant vigor is still revived the hymn of Charles Wesley, with the added charm of Mendelssohn music:

Hark! The herald angels sing
Glory to the King of Kings!
        Peace on earth and mercy mild,

        God and sinners reconciled!
Joyful, all ye nations, rise,
Join the triumph of the skies;
Universal Nature say,
Christ, the Lord, is born today!

Any collection of Christmas poems will contain the name of Robert Herrick, the Vicar of Dean Prior, Devonshire, from 1629 until 1662, omitting the fifteen years when he was banished by Puritan rule. "Noble Numbers," and though they are less familiar than his lays of love and domestic life, they contain five worthy carols, among them the one beginning, "What sweeter music can we bring?" sung to the King at Whitehall.

On a loftier plane of poetry than his contemporaries could achieve or appreciate, Milton, at twenty-one, wrote his Ode and Hymn on the Nativity, a Christmas poem whose organ melody and majestic sentiment outrank all similar efforts in any literature. The grandeur of this Christmas hymn may best be realized by a comparative reading of the lesser poems of the same class and time, the Hymns on the Nativity by Ben Jonson, John Donne, Richard Crawshaw, George Herbert and Jeremy Taylor. Many of these carols consisted of pictures of the shepherds and their dialogue on the night of revelation. Succeeding the hymns of the Puritan era, often sung to joyful music, as already cited, came a return to the more distinctive carol form, as a lay of triumph and adoration. The last century produced many such poems, of high literary quality and, in many cases, adapted by latter-day composers to stately, noble church music. Beside the Easter carols, these Christmas odes have found a permanent place, where, amid worshipful and dignified surroundings, they serve both as a reminiscence of past custom and also as an educative medium for both aesthetic and spiritual faculties by their beauty of form and ennobling ideals.

In Coleridge's carol, "The Shepherds Went their Hasty Way," we note, in its finale, the grand, oft-quoted couplet, text for many a later ode:

Joy rise in me, like a summer's morn,
Peace, Peace on Earth! The Prince of Peace is born!

Wordsworth's "Christmas Minstrelsy," like the familiar passage in "Marmion," is reminiscent of the ancient Christmas customs; it was dedicated to his brother, Rev. Christopher Wordsworth, from whose pen came one of the most graceful, rhythmic carols, still familiar to ear and voice:

Hark! the sound of Holy Voices
    Chanting o'er the Crystal Sea,
Alleluia, Alleluia,
Alleluia, Lord to Thee!

The name of Bishop Heber suggests his alliterative, melodious carol, dated 1811, "Brightest and Best of the Stars of the Morning." Deep, religious fervor characterizes the less familiar carols by Mrs. Hemans, Charles Kingsley and Christina Rossetti. The latter's poem is most unique, with her peculiar union of mysticism and realism, while it is, as well, suggestive of the later spirit of adoration through heart service and commemorative gifts:

In the bleak mid-winter
Frosty winds made moan,
Earth stood hard as iron,
Water like a stone;
Snow had fallen, snow on snow,
Snow on snow,
In the bleak mid-winter
Long ago.

Our God, heaven cannot hold Him,
Nor earth sustain;
Heaven and earth shall flee away
When He comes to reign;
In the bleak mid-winter
A stable-place sufficed
The Lord God Almighty
Jesus Christ.

Enough for Him whom cherubim
Worship night and day,
A breastful of milk
And a mangerful of hay;
Enough for Him whom angels
Fall down before,
The ox and ass and camel
Which adore.
Angels and archangels

May have gathered there.
Cherubim and seraphim
Thronged the air;
But only His mother,
In her maiden bliss,
Worshipped the Beloved
With a kiss.

What can I give Him,
Poor as I am?
If I were a shepherd,
I would bring a lamb;
If I were a wise man,
I would do my part —
Yet what I can I give Him:
Give my heart

The Pre-Raphaelite school have furnished three carols full of
melody and picturesqueness; Swinburne's "Three Damsels in the

Queen's Chamber," suggested by Rossetti's drawing, has a medieval charm, and in its refrains suggests the older carol-motive:

> Mary, most full of grace,
> Bring us to thy Son's face.
> ✳✳✳✳✳
>
> Mary, that is most wise,
> Bring us to thy Son's eyes.

William Morris introduced Christmas carols and odes into his romantic "Defence of Guinevere" and his allegorical "The Earthly Paradise." Yet more familiar is his Nowell carol, "Masters, in this Hall." Always apt and popular are the Christmas lullaby songs; among recent "rocking carols," none surpass in grace and peaceful suggestion John Addington Symonds' lullaby picture.

Among Longfellow's translations or adaptations is one of the most ancient Noels, while to familiar music we still sing Whittier's "Christmas Carmen":

> Sound over all waters, reach out from all lands,
> The chorus of voices, the clasping of hands;
> Sing hymns that were sung by the stars of the morn!
> Sing songs of the angels when Jesus was born!

Among the worthy customs of the past, decadent today, this of carol writing and carol-singing has been mentioned as matter of special regret. Even a cursory review of the poetry and music of the last fifty years, however, testifies to the maintenance of the carol, as a form of worshipful, exultant verse. It has firm root in the hearts of the race, as expression of the greatest event in religious history; it has also perennial charm as a form of poetry and song. Under the transformed conditions of modern life, carol singing in the streets would lose the purity and picturesqueness of the past ages, and might suffer degradation and license in revival of the more secular themes. The carol today maintains place and finds favor in the church, the school and the home, where, amid peaceful, lofty influences, it best retains its pristine and worshipful incentive. Moreover, while the modern poet and chorister are true to the technique of the flexible carol of the past, both in theme and music, the potent sentiments of current thought and life, the trend toward fraternity and altruism, the reverence for labor of head and hand, the interpretation of the gospel of love as the gospel of service — such ideals are interwoven with the ever-present adoration and joy.

Last year was published a carol, "Ave Jesu" by Dean Stubbs, a felicitous revival of the old-time forms of diction and structure, rendered yet more effective by the noble, exultant music composed by the chorister of York Minster. A note, appended, stated that the words were written in "the late Bishop Phillips Brooks' old study in Trinity Rectory, Boston." More inspiratory environment could never have been found for embodiment both of the worship of our fathers and the aims of modern Christian and Christmas service. Among Bishop Brooks' own poems is a carol, whose benign grace and magnetic message form fitting expression of his own aspirations and the wide, dominant note of joyance at this later Christmastide:

Everywhere, everywhere, Christmas tonight!
Christmas in lands of the fir-tree and pine,
Christmas in lands of the palm-tree and vine;
Christmas where snow-peaks stand solemn and white,
Christmas where cornfields lie sunny and bright;
Everywhere, everywhere, Christmas tonight!
Christmas where children are hopeful and gay,
Christmas where old men are patient and grey;
Christmas where peace, like a dove in its flight,
Broods o'er brave men in the thick of the fight;
Everywhere, everywhere, Christmas tonight!

For the Christ-Child who is Master of all,
No palace too great and no cottage too small.
The angels who welcome Him sing from the height,
"In the city of David a King in His might,"
Everywhere, everywhere, Christmas tonight!

CHRISTMAS CAROLS

*****

So the stars of the midnight which compass us round
Shall see a strange glory and hear a sweet sound,
And cry, "Look, the earth is aflame with delight!"
O sons of the morning, rejoice at the sight,
Everywhere, everywhere, Christmas tonight!

The Christmas Barring-Out.

From 'The Gentleman's Magazine," November 1828

IT WAS a few days before the usual period of the Christmas holidays arrived, when the leading scholars of the head form determined on reviving the ancient but almost obsolete custom of barring-out the matter of the school. Many years had elapsed since the attempt had succeeded; and many times since that period had it been made in vain. The scholars had heard of the glorious fetes of their forefathers in their boyish years, when they set the lash of the master at defiance for days together. Now, alas! All was changed; the master, in the opinion of the boys, reigned a despot absolute and uncontrolled. The merciless cruelty of his rod, and the heaviness of his tasks, were insupportable. The accustomed holidays bad been rescinded; the usual Christmas feast reduced to a non-entity, and the chartered rights of the scholars were continually violated. These grievances were discussed seriatim; and we all were unanimously of opinion that our wrongs should, if possible, be redressed. But how the object should be effected was a momentous and weighty affair. The master was a clergyman of the old school, who for the last forty years had exercised an authority hitherto uncontrolled, and who had no idea of enforcing scholastic discipline without the exercise of the whip. The consequences of a failure were terrible to reflect upon; but then, the anticipation of success, and the glory attendant upon the enterprise, if successful, were sufficient to dispel every fear.

At the head of the Greek class there was one whose very soul seemed formed for the most daring attempts. He communicated his intentions to a chosen few, of which the writer was one, and offered to be the leader of the undertaking, if we would promise him our support. We hesitated; but he represented the certainty of success with such feeling eloquence, that he entirely subdued our opposition. He stated that Addison had acquired immortal fame by a similar enterprise. He told us that almost every effort in the sacred cause of freedom had succeeded. He appealed to our classical recollections; — Epaminondas and Leonidas were worthy of our example; — Tarquin and Caesar, as tyrants, had fallen before the united efforts of freedom; we had only to be unanimous, and the rod of this scholastic despot would be forever broken. We then entered enthusiastically into his views. He observed that delays were dangerous; the "barring-out," he said, "should take place the very next morning, to prevent the possibility of being betrayed." On a previous occasion (he said) some officious little urchin had told the master the whole plot — several days having been allowed to intervene between the planning of the project and its execution; and to the astonishment of the boys, it appeared they found the master at his desk two hours before his usual time, and had the mortification of being congratulated on their early attendance, with an order to be there every morning at the same hour!

To prevent the recurrence of such a defeat, we determined on organizing our plans that very night. The boys were accordingly told to assemble after school hours at a well-known tombstone, in the neighboring Churchyard, as something of importance was under consideration. The place of meeting was an elevated parallelogram tombstone, which had always served as a kind of council-table to settle our little disputes, as well as parties of pleasure. Here we all assembled at the appointed time. Our leader took his stand at one end of the stone, with the head-boys who were in the secret, on each side of him. "My boys, (he laconically observed) tomorrow morning we are to *bar out* the flogging parson; and to make him promise that he will not flog us hereafter without a cause; nor set us long tasks, or deprive us of our holidays. The boys of the Greek form will be your Captains, and I am to be your Captain general. Those who are cowards had better retire, and be satisfied with future floggings; hut you who have courage, and know what it is to have been flogged for nothing, come here and sign your names." He immediately pulled out a pen and a sheet of paper; and having tied some bits of thread round the finger ends of two or three boys, with a pin he drew blood to answer for ink, and to give more solemnity to the act. He signed the first, the Captains next, and the rest in succession. Many of the lesser boys slunk away during the ceremony; but on counting the names we found we mustered upwards of forty — sufficient, it was imagined, even to carry the school by storm. The Captain-general then addressed us: — "I have the key of the school, and shall be there at seven o'clock. The old Parson will arrive at nine, and every one of you must be there before eight, to allow us one hour for barricading the doors and windows. Bring with you as much provision as you can; and tell your parents that you have to take your dinners in school. Let every one of you have some weapon of defense; you who cannot obtain a sword, pistol, or poker, must bring a stick or cudgcl. Now all go home directly, and be sure to arrive early in the morning."

Perhaps a more restless and anxious night was never passed by young recruits on the eve of a general battle. Many of us rose some hours before the time; and at seven o'clock, when the school-door was opened, there was a tolerably numerous muster. Our Captain immediately ordered candles to be lighted, and a rousing fire to be made (for it was a dark December's morning). He then began to examine the store of provisions, and the arms which each had brought. In the meantime, the arrival of every boy with additional material, was announced by tremendous cheers.

THE CHRISTMAS BARRING-OUT

At length the Church clock struck eight. "Proceed to barricade the doors and windows (exclaimed the Captain), or the old lion will be upon us before we are prepared to meet him." In an instant the old oaken door rang on its heavy hinges. Some, with hammers, gimlets, and nails, were eagerly securing the windows, while others were dragging along the ponderous desks, forms, and everything portable, to blockade, with certain security, every place which might admit of ingress. This operation being completed, the Captain mounted the master's rostrum, and called over the list of names, when he found only two or three missing. He then proceeded to classify them into divisions or companies of six, and assigned to each its respective Captain. He prescribed the duties of each company. Two were to guard the large casement window, where, it was expected, the first attack would be made; this was considered the post of honor, and consequently the strongest boys, with the most formidable weapons, were selected, whom we called Grenadiers. Another company, whom we considered as the Light Infantry, or Sharp Shooters, were ordered to mount a large desk in the center of the school; and, armed with squibs, crackers, and various missiles, they were to attack the enemy over the heads of the combatants. The other divisions were to guard the back windows and door, and to act according to the emergency of the moment. Our leader then moved some resolutions (which in imitation of Brutus he had cogitated during the previous night), to the effect that each individual should implicitly obey his own Captain, that each Captain should follow the orders of the Captain-general, and that a corps de reserve should be stationed in the rear, to enforce this obedience, and prevent the combatants from taking to flight. The resolutions were passed amidst loud vociferations.[1]

---

1   In Miss Edgeworth's collection of Juvenile Stories, there is a little interesting sketch, called the Barring-out, or Party Spirit. The scene is given at a private boarding school. "The arrangement of the affair," she observes, "was left to the new manager, to whom all pledged implicit obedience. Obedience, it seems, is necessary, even from rebels to their ring leaders — not reasonable but implicit obedience." — "Archer [the name of the captain, or manager, as she calls him] and his associates agreed to stay the last in the

We next commenced an examination of the various weapons, and found them to consist of one old blunderbuss, one pistol, two old swords, a few rusty pokers, and slicks, stones, squibs, and gunpowder in abundance. The firearms were immediately loaded with blank powder; the swords were sharpened, and the pokers heated in the fire. These weapons were assigned to the most daring company, who had to protect the principal window. The missiles were for the light infantry, and all the rest were armed with sticks.

We now began to maneuver our companies, by marching them into line and column, so that every one might know his own situation. In the midst of this preparation the sentinel, whom we had placed at the window, loudly vociferated, "The parson! The parson's coming!"

In an instant all was confusion. Every one ran he knew not where; as if eager to fly, or screen himself from observation. Our captain instantly mounted a form, and called to the captains of the two leading companies to take their stations. They immediately obeyed; and the other companies followed their example; though they found it much more difficult to maneuver when danger approached, than they had a few minutes before! The well-known footstep, which bad often struck on our ears with terror, was now heard to advance along the portico. The master tried to lift the latch again and again in vain. The muttering of his stern voice sounded on our ears like the lion's growl. A deathlike silence prevailed. We scarcely dared to breathe. The palpitations of our little hearts could perhaps alone be heard. The object of our dread then went round to the front window, for the

schoolroom, and as soon as the Greybeards [a name given to an opposing party of boys] were gone out to bed, he, as a signal, was to shut and lock one door, and Townsend the other; a third conspirator was to strike a light, in case they should not be able to secure a candle; a fourth was to take charge of the candle as soon as lighted, and all the rest were to run to the bars, which were secreted in the room; then to fix them to the common fastening bars of the window, in the manner in which they had been previously instructed by the manager. Thus each had his part assigned, and each was warned that the success of the whole depended upon their order and punctuality. Order and punctuality, it appears, are necessary even in a barring-out; and even rebellion must have its laws."

purpose of ascertaining whether any one was in the school. Every footstep struck us with awe; not a word, not a whisper was heard. He approached close to the window; and with an astonished countenance stood gazing upon us, while we were ranged in battle array, motionless as statues, and silent as the tomb. "What is the meaning of this?"' he impatiently exclaimed. But no answer could he obtain; for who would then have dared to render himself conspicuous by a reply? Pallid countenances and livid lips betrayed our fears. The courage which one hour before was ready to brave every danger, appeared to be fled. Everyone seemed anxious to conceal himself from view; and there would certainly have been a general flight through the back windows, had it not been for the prudent regulation of a corps-de-reserve, armed with cudgels, to prevent it.

"You young scoundrels, open the door instantly," he again exclaimed; and what added to our indescribable horror, in a fit of rage he dashed his hand through the window, which consisted of small diamond-shaped panes, and appeared as if determined to force his way in.

Fear and trepidation, attended by an increasing commotion, now possessed us all. At this critical moment every eye turned to our captain, as if to reproach him for having brought us into this terrible dilemma. He alone stood unmoved; but he saw that none would have courage to obey his commands. Some exciting stimulus was necessary. Suddenly waving his hand, he exclaimed aloud, "Three cheers for the barring-out, and success to our cause!" [Hurrah! Hurrah! Hurrah!] The cheers were tremendous. Our courage revived; the blood flushed in our cheeks; the parson was breaking in; the moment was critical. Our captain undaunted sprang to the fireplace — seized a heated poker in one hand, and a blazing torch in the other. The latter he gave to the captain of the sharp-shooters, and told him to prepare a volley; when with the red-hot poker he fearlessly advanced to the window-seat; and daring his master to enter, he ordered an attack, — and an attack indeed was made, sufficiently tremendous to have repelled a more powerful assailant. The missiles flew at the ill-fated window from every quarter. The blunderbuss and the pistol were fired; squibs and crackers, inkstands and rulers, stones, and even burning coals, came in showers about the casement, and broke some of the panes into a thousand pieces; while blazing torches, healed pokers, and sticks, stood bristling under the window. The whole was scarcely the work of a minute. The astonished master reeled back in dumb amazement. He had evidently been struck with a missile, or with the broken glass; and probably fancied he was wounded by the firearms. The school now rang with the shouts of "victory," and continued cheering. "The enemy again approaches," cries the captain; "Fire another volley; stay; he seeks a parley, hear him." — "What is the meaning, I say, of this horrid tumult?" "The barring-out, the barring-out!" a dozen voices instantly exclaimed. "For shame," says he, in a tone evidently subdued, "what disgrace you are bringing upon yourselves and the school. What will the Trustees — what will your parents say? William (continued he, addressing the captain,) open the door without further delay." — "I will, Sir," he replied, "on your promising to pardon us, and to give us our lawful holidays, of which we have lately been deprived; and not set us tasks during the holidays." "Yes, yes," said several squealing voices, "that is what we want; and not to be flogged for nothing." "You insolent scoundrels! You consummate young villains!" he exclaimed, choking with rage, and at the same time making a furious effort to break through the already shattered window, "open the door instantly, or I'll break every bone in your hides." "Not on those conditions," replied our captain, with provoking coolness; — "come on, my boys; another volley." No sooner said than done, and even with more fury than before. Like men driven to despair, who expect no quarter on surrendering, the little urchins daringly mounted the window-seat, which was a broad old-fashioned one, and pointed the firearms and heated poker at him; whilst others advanced with the squibs and missiles. "Come on, my lads," says the captain, "let this be our Thermopylae, and I will be your Leonidas." And indeed so daring were they, that each seemed ready to emulate the Spartans of old. The master, perceiving their determined obstinacy, turned round without further remonstrance, and indignantly walked away.

Relieved from our terrors, we now became intoxicated with joy. The walls rang with repeated hurrahs! In the madness of enthusiasm some of the boys began to tear up the forms, throw the books about, break the slates, locks, and cupboards, and act so outrageously that the captain called them to order; not, however, before the master's desk and drawers had been broken open, and every plaything, which had been taken from the scholars, restored to its owner.

We now began to think of provisions. They were all placed on one table, and dealt out in rations by the captain of each company. In the meantime we held a council of war, as we called it, to determine on what was to be done.

In a recess at the east end of the school, there stood a large oak chest, black with age, whose heavy hinges had become corroded with years of rust. It was known to contain the records and endowments of the school, and, as we presumed, the regulations for the treatment of the scholars. The oldest boy had never seen its inside. Attempts, dictated by insatiable curiosity, had often been made to open it; but it was deemed impregnable. It was guarded by three immense locks, and each key was in the possession of different persons. The wood appeared to be nearly half a foot thick, and every corner was plaited with iron. All eyes were instinctively directed to this mysterious chest. Could any means be devised for effecting an entrance? was the natural question. We all proceeded to reconnoiter. We attempted to move it, but in vain. We made some feeble efforts to force the lid; it was firm as a block of marble. At length one daring urchin brought from the fireplace a red-hot poker, and began to bore through its sides. A universal shout was given. Other pokers were brought, and to work they went. The smoke and tremendous smell, which the old wood sent forth rather alarmed us. We were apprehensive that we might burn the records, instead of obtaining a copy of them. This arrested our progress for a few minutes.

At this critical moment a shout was set up that the parson and a constable were coming! Down went the pokers, and, as if conscience-stricken, we were all seized with consternation. The casement window was so shattered, that it could easily be entered by any resolute fellow. In the desperation of the moment we seized the desks, forms, and stools, to block it up; but our courage in some degree had evaporated; and we felt reluctant to act on the offensive. The old gentleman and his attendant deliberately inspected the windows and fastenings; but, without making any attempt to enter, they retreated, for the purpose, as we presumed, of obtaining additional assistance. What was now to be done? The master appeared obdurate; and we had gone too far to recede. Some proposed to drill a hole in the window-seat, fill it with gunpowder, and explode it, if anyone attempted to enter. Others thought we had better prepare to set fire to the school sooner than surrender unconditionally. But the majority advised what was perhaps the most prudent resolution, to wait for another attack; and, if we saw no hopes of sustaining a longer defense, to make the best retreat we could.

The affair of the Barring-out had now become known, and persons began to assemble round the windows, calling out that the master was coming with assistants, and saying everything to intimidate us. Many of us were completely jaded with the over-excitement we had experienced since the previous evening. The school was hot, close, and full of smoke. Some were longing for liberty and fresh air; and most of us were now of opinion that we had engaged in an affair, which it was impossible to accomplish. In this state of mind we received another visit from our dreaded master. With his stick he commenced a more furious attack than before; and observing us less turbulent, he appeared determined to force his way, in spite of the barricades. The younger boys thought of nothing but flight and self-preservation; and the rush to the back-windows became general. In the midst of this consternation our captain exclaims, "Let us not fly like cowards; if we must surrender, let the gates of the citadel be thrown open; the day is against us; but let us bravely face the enemy, and march out with the honors of war." Some few had already escaped; but the rest immediately ranged themselves on each side the school, in two extended lines, with their weapons in hand. The door was thrown open — the master instantly entered, and passed between the two lines, denouncing vengeance on us all. But as he marched in, we marched out in military order; and giving three cheers, we dispersed into the neighboring fields.

We shortly met again, and after a little consultation, it was determined that none of the leaders should come to school until sent for, and a free pardon given.

The defection, however, was so general, that no corporal punishments took place. Many of the boys did not return till after the holidays; and several of the elder ones never entered the school again.

On the Custom
of Barring-Out

O f the many strange customs which prevailed among our medieval ancestors, and which of late years have rapidly fallen into desuetude, that of *Barring-out*, as it is called, appears the most irreconcilable to the habits and sentiments of modern times. To a scholastic disciplinarian of the Metropolis, the custom would appear outrageous, and almost incredulous. It reminds us of the Roman Saturnalia of old, when masters, for a certain time, were subservient to their servants and slaves.

Hutchinson, in his History of Cumberland, Vol. 2. p. 322, when speaking of the parish of Bromfield, thus adverts to the practice of Barring-out:

"Till within the last twenty or thirty years, it had been a custom, time out of mind, for the scholars of the Free-school of Bromfield, about the beginning of Lent, or in the more expressive phraseology of the country, at Fasting's Even, to bar out the master; i.e. to depose and exclude him from his school, and keep him out for three days. During the period of this expulsion, the doors of the citadel, the school, were strongly barricaded within: and the boys, who defended it like a besieged city, were armed, in general, with bore-tree, or elder popguns. The master, meanwhile, made various efforts, both by force and stratagem, to regain his lost authority. If he succeeded, heavy tasks were imposed, and the business of the school was resumed and submitted to; but it more commonly happened that he was repulsed and defeated. After three days' siege, terms of capitulation were proposed by the master, and accepted by the boys. These terms were summed up in an old formula of Latin Leonine verses; stipulating what hours and times should, for the year ensuing, be allotted to study, and what to relaxation and play. Securities were provided by each side for the due performance of these stipulations: and the paper was then solemnly signed both by master and scholars."

Brand, when noticing the subject in his Popular Antiquities, quotes the above passage from Hutchinson, and says, it was "a custom that having now fallen into disuse, will soon be totally forgotten." Brand was certainly mistaken in this assertion. In Cumberland the custom still prevails, and is not likely soon to be forgotten. To my certain knowledge it has taken place at Scotby, Wetherall, Warwick, etc. within the last ten years; and I understand that the practice is still occasionally enforced. I have been informed by a young friend, who left Scotby School a very few years ago, that he had been frequently engaged in these affairs. He stated that when the master was barred-out, the written orders for the holidays, etc. were put through the keyhole of the school door, with a request for the master to sign them, which, after some hesitation and a few threats, he generally consented to. On one occasion, however, he forced his way through the window; but was instantly expelled, vi et armis, and his coattail burnt to pieces by squibs and blazing paper.

Brand mentions the custom as being very prevalent in the city of Durham, and other places in the county; as Houghton-le-Spring, Thornton, etc.

A writer in your Magazine, Vol. 61. p. 1170, mentioning some local customs of Westmoreland and Cumberland, remarks,

"In September or October, the master is locked out of the school by the scholars, who, previous to his admittance, give an account of the different holidays for the ensuing year, which he promises to observe, and signs his name to the Orders, as they are called, with two bondsmen. The return of these signed Orders is the signal of capitulation; the doors are immediately opened; beef, beer, and wine, deck the festive board; and the day is spent in mirth."

Dr. Johnson, in his life of Addison, says,

"In 1683, when Addison had entered his twelfth year, his father, now become Dean of Litchfield, committed him to the care of Mr. Shaw, master of the grammar school in that city. While he was under the tuition of Shaw, his enterprise and courage have been recorded in leading and conducting successfully a plan for barring-out his master, a disorderly privilege which, in his time, prevailed in the principal seminaries of education, where the boys, exulting at the approach of their periodical liberty, and unwilling to wait its regular commencement, took possession of the school some days before the time of regular recess, of which they barred the door; and, not contented with the exclusive occupation of the fortress, usually bade their master defiance from the windows. The whole operation of this practice was, at Litchfield, planned and conducted by Addison."

Though the masters, in many cases, evidently submitted to this outrageous custom, in other places it was resisted and put down, as we may see from the following extract, which appears among the statutes of the grammar school founded at Kilkenny, in Ireland, March 18, 1684, and copied into Vallancey's Collectanea de rebus Hibernicis, Vol. 2, p. 512:

"In the number of stubborn and refractory lads, who shall refuse to submit to the orders and correction of the said school, who are to be forthwith dismissed, and not readmitted without due submission to exemplary punishment, and on the second offense to be discharged and expelled forever, are reckoned such as shall offer to shut out the master or usher; but the master shall give them leave to break up eight days before Christmas, and three days before Easter and Whitsuntide."

Though this custom has attracted the notice of different writers, 1 am not aware that a detailed account has ever been given to the world by anyone engaged in such an affair. The preparations, the consultations, the anxieties attendant on an undertaking so all-important to a boyish mind, would have been deserving the pen of an Addison, who was himself the main spring, as Johnson informs us, in one of these daring affairs.

The custom used to prevail in some parts of Lancashire; but the last attempt at a barring-out, of which I have ever heard in that county, was at the Free Grammar-school of Ormskirk,[2] in which the writer of the following simple detail was actively engaged; and I am sure no publication is more calculated to transmit a correct knowledge of such a custom to posterity than the imperishable pages of the *Gentleman's Magazine*. Whilst some may be ready to exclaim, "could such things be?" others, who have witnessed them, may recall to mind a thousand delightful reminiscences connected with the early period of scholastic life.

---

2   The Grammar-school of Ormskirk was erected in 1614, by Henry Croft, esq. The emoluments of the headmaster, arising from certain endowments, amount to about 200l. per annum; and he receives from each scholar a stated sum at Michaelmas, Christmas, and Candlemas, respectively. The scholars are admitted on the recommendation of a visiting trustee, of which the Vicar of the parish is one. They are always expected to learn the Latin and Greek languages. Writing, arithmetic, etc. are taught at an extra expense. The headmaster must necessarily be a clergyman, who holds at the same time the perpetual curacy of Altcar, about five miles from Ormskirk. The Rev. W. Naylor, whose death was recorded in Vol. 92. i. p. 380, was head of the school for upwards of half a century. The Rev. Mr. Forshaw is the present master. Of late years the original intention of the founder (with respect to the tuition being confined to classical learning) has been much neglected; and I believe that the half-yearly visits of the trustees, at which the boys were strictly examined, have been long discontinued.

The Passing of the Christmas Ghost Story.

BY STEPHEN LEACOCK

From 'The Bookman' magazine, November 1919

IT IS a nice question whether Christmas, in the good old sense of the term, is not passing away from us. One associates it somehow with the epoch of stagecoaches, of gabled inns and hospitable country homes with the flames roaring in the open fireplaces. To appreciate a Christmas gathering one must have fought one's way to it on horseback through ten miles of driving snow, or ridden in an ancient closed coach wheel-deep in melting slush. To arrive off a suburban trolley, punctual to the minute, won't do. Somehow the magic is out of it. I often think that half the charm of Christmas, in literature at least, lay in the rough weather and in the physical difficulties surmounted by the sheer force of the glad spirit of the day. Take, for example, the immortal Christmases of Mr. Pickwick and his friends at Dingley Dell and the uncounted thousands of Christmas guests of that epoch of which they were the type. The snow blustered about them. They were red and ruddy with the flush of a strenuous journey. Great fires must be lighted in the expectation of their coming. Huge tankards of spiced ale must be warmed up for them. There must be red wine basking to a ruddier glow in the firelight. There must be warm slippers and hot cordials and a hundred and one little comforts to think of as a mark of gratitude for their arrival; and behind it all, the lurking fear that some fierce highwayman might have fallen upon them as they rode in the darkness of the wood.

Take as against this a Christmas in a New York apartment with the guests arriving by the subway and the elevator, or with no greater highwayman to fear than the taxicab driver. Warm them up with spiced ale? They're not worth it.

Can one wonder, then, that the older "literature of Christmas" is passing away? And most of all, the good old Christmas ghost story, parent of a thousand terrors. How well one recalls its awful apparatus — its "figures" and its "apparitions," the "hollow voice" in which they spoke and the way in which, as the culminating terror, the figure "disappeared through the wall"! A humble trick it seems in these days to eyes that have watched Charlie Chaplin run up the side of a ten-story building and disappear into the sky.

Yet the people of the Victorian age, when ghost stories were ghost stories, loved nothing better than to get round a blazing fire as the night grew late and listen to a tale of "apparitions" and "figures" till even the stoutest of them took up his tallow candle to go to bed in a fit of the shudders, or, more dreadful and more delicious still, to read the awful tale in bed itself and by the uncertain light of the taper.

How well one recalls the opening and the setting of such an old-time ghost story.

"I am not what one would call a nervous man," so the story used to begin, "yet there was something in the gloomy aspect of Buggam Grange, as one approached it from the dark avenue of silent spruce trees, that might well strike a chill, etc., etc."

And how well one remembers this Buggam Grange! Evening is always "just falling" as one approaches it. The wind is "soughing" among its ancient chimneys. The house is wrapped in darkness save for a dim light here and there that struggles (I think "struggles" is the word) through the casement of a closed window. The "East

Wing" — the very name invites a shudder at once — stands gloomy and untenanted.

Such is Buggam Grange as we approach it upon our wearied horse. No, we are not nervous but Buggam Grange more or less "puts us to the bad" at sight. Yet imagine how different if we came buzzing up to Buggam Grange in a hundred-horse-power car: if Buggam Grange had electric light streaming out of its windows. Moaning of the wind! One would never hear it in the noise of the car. Or what if one did? One would merely ask to use the telephone for a minute and call up the emergency plumber of Buggam Hampstead and say: "Hullo, this is Buggam Grange speaking. The wind is soughing rather badly round one of our chimney tops. Will you please send up a man? Thank you."

But in the days of the great darkness, before electricity was, Buggam Grange was a fearsome place indeed. Note our mode of entry to it. The door is unchained and we are admitted by a "solitary servant"; he is the "faithful butler" of the Buggam family: he has been in their service as boy and man for fifty years: he shakes his aged head with mournful foreboding as he lights us to our room in the dreaded East Wing. No one has slept in it for fifty years: none, in fact, since that dreadful night fifty years ago — and it was, by the strangest of coincidences, also a Christmas Eve — when Sir Duggam Buggam stabbed his best friend in the Tower room over a game of cards. If it had been auction bridge we could have understood it, if he had stabbed all his best friends. But when we remember it was cribbage, it seems hard to understand. Yet they hanged Sir Duggam for his crime at the assizes fifty years ago, and the villagers in Buggam Hampstead still tell strange stories of lights seen and voices heard in the East Wing of the Grange at Christmas time!

Can you wonder that when we are lighted to bed in that very Tower room, and remember this is Christmas Eve — exactly fifty years after the murder, not forty-nine, fifty — something nearly approaching to a shudder goes through us? As for that aged butler who says good night to us with "another melancholy shake of his head" (it is his one stunt), any reader of Christmas ghost stories knows what happens to him. He will be found dead, of course, next morning, stretched upon the floor of his pantry. Don't ask me what is going to kill him. It will never be known. That was the dreadful thing about these Buggam Grange stories. There was no explanation given. The faithful butler was found dead stretched at full length (not half-length or foreshortened in any way, full length) upon the floor. These, one must remember, were the days before Sherlock Holmes. Sherlock would have made short work of the butler. He would have tracked the marks that his boots had made on the cement floor of the pantry, and "solved" him in no time.

But I am anticipating in talking of the dead butler. He is not found till the morning. Let us turn to consider the things that used, in the old-fashioned ghost stories, to happen to ourselves in the haunted room in the East Wing. How familiar all the old mechanism sounds: and how silly it has all grown in the bright light of electricity.

We try in vain to compose ourselves to sleep. Somehow we can't sleep. Can one really wonder at it? In a damp old room with the wind soughing all over the place and the casement rattling and our ghastly "night light" (an invention of the devil used in the Victorian Age) throwing vast flickering shadows upon the ceiling. And the tapestry against the walls — I forgot the tapestry — moving slightly in the night wind! Put a modern reader in a room with those things and he'd leap out of bed in a frenzy, turn on the electric light, and grab the telephone and call for two plumbers and an upholsterer.

But in the Victorian days of the ghost story these things were denied. We had to lie in bed and tremble until at last we fall into a "fitful slumber."

Do we know how long we have slept? We don't. All that we know is that we are awakened by a sound that comes "from behind the wainscot" — a groaning. Our night-light has flickered out. The room is in darkness and there is no electric switch. And someone is groaning behind the wainscot! We are not, generally speaking, a nervous man, but we confess now to "a feeling of apprehension." Oh, yes.

We lie there. We have to: there is nothing else that we can do. And then somehow we become aware of a "presence" in the room. We do not see it or hear it or smell it, but we "become aware of it." This presence which figured in all the ghost stories of the old days, has now been overwhelmed and forgotten in the litter of new psycho-spiritual jargon: it has been replaced by "phantasms" and "phantograms" and such. But I do believe it was worse and more terrible when it was labeled simply a "presence." And we have become aware of it! The only thing is, has it become aware of us? Great Heavens, let us hope it hasn't.

Ah, but it has, it has! Look what happens next! It is now no longer merely a "presence." It has become a "figure." This is worse. A "figure," thin and impalpable as the night air, is moving about the room. It is illuminated by a "spectral light." It moves nearer to our bedside. It extends its hand. Oh, help! And now it is no longer a "figure." It has become an "apparition" — look! It is the apparition of Sir Duggam Buggam! The face is "grave and sad." Apparitions' faces always are: it is something in the life they lead that does it. The apparition points with its shadowy hand to the ghastly mark about its neck, the mark left by the hangman's noose. We can feel our hair rise on end, on both ends, and then — "a prolonged and ghastly shriek is heard to resound from somewhere in the house below."

This is enough. We quit. In the words of the original stories "our senses leave us" and we "know no more."

When we awake, the "bright sun" is streaming in at the windows, and the birds (who would have thought that there were birds at Buggam Grange!) are singing outside the window.

"Workmen entering the house in the morning" (luckily they never went on strike then) find the body of the butler. Then the whole ghastly story comes out. Sir Duggam was innocent of the "foul deed." It was the butler, then a young man of twenty-five, who had stabbed the guest for the sake of the gold piled upon the cribbage table. Sir Duggam was found, insensible still from drink, beside the body. His protests were in vain. He was hanged. Note that in Victorian literature the fact that Sir Duggam was "insensible from drink" — now called "spiflocated" — was not held to his discredit. The butler's confession hidden away in a drawer of his pantry made all clear.

As to what killed the butler, or who gave the shriek, or what the apparition was doing in the room, don't ask me. These things came and went as vaguely and as inconsistently as the flickering of the night-light. Explanations only spoil a story, anyway.

Such was the kind of stuff at which the Victorian reader loved to shudder. I have before me as I write a little, forgotten volume published in 1852, and labeled the "Night Side of Nature" by Catherine Crowe. A whole generation has shivered over its pages, blown out its bedside candle, and buried its head under the clothes in fear. Miss Crowe — or no, she must have been Mrs. Crowe; such a woman would have been snapped up like Scheherezade — spares her readers no horror. She won't even label her characters by their names in ordinary Christian fashion. Here, for instance, is a dreadful tale concerning "the uncle of a Greek gentleman, Mr. M—, traveling in Magnesia." I confess that the very name is too much for me. I admit that I'd hate to be away off in the heart of "Magnesia" with a Greek called M—. This story (I dare not read it, the beginning is enough) is in a chapter headed "Troubled Spirits." What do you know about that? And here is another chapter called "Haunted Houses," and a still more terrible looking one headed "Miscellaneous Phenomena." No man I think can be blamed for admitting that he lives in deadly fear of miscellaneous phenomena. We all do.

And now why is it that the ghost story should have passed away, or rather, why did it flourish just at the time when it did? Here, I think, is the reason. The ghost story flourished best at that period (the middle of the nineteenth century) because at that period people had lost the belief in ghosts, at least as a serious, everyday part of their creed. The wonderful revelations of natural science were hurrying the thinking world in a cheap and vainglorious materialism: an apparition was dismissed as a mere "phosphorescence" — a vastly different thing; a noise behind a wainscot was a rat; a "sense of melancholy foreboding" was a stomachache. Everything was known and labeled and assigned to its true place in the universe — except perhaps two or three awkward little problems which were bunched together as the "unknowable" and shoved into a corner.

In such a world there was no room for ghosts. Hence a ghost story was not a true story. It was a wild reversion of the imagination to the forgotten terrors of the past. In earlier days, in the Middle Ages, let us say, this was not so. A ghost story was a true story. It might be very terrible, yet it was after all merely a statement of terrible fact, not a wild terror of the imagination. If a man related that an evil spirit had appeared to him in the night, he meant exactly what he said. It was a plain statement of a distressing fact. It was just as if a man said nowadays that his tailor had turned up at his house in the day — the same sort of thing. It was a bothersome thing and might mean a lot of trouble to come, but there was nothing in the relation of it that involved the wide-eyed terror of the nineteenth century. The materialist, in his horrors of the night, paid the penalty of his vainglory by day.

And now the scene has changed again. The ghosts have all come back. They are buzzing round us all the time. Oliver Lodge and Conan Doyle have seen bunches of them. They think nothing of them. It appears that one can talk to them by telepathy, or by table-rapping, or with a Ouija board or in a dozen ways: and then when one does, their poor minds are so enfeebled from living behind the wainscot that one can feel nothing but pity for their simple talk. One respects them in a way: they are a religious lot: they like to talk of how bright and beautiful it is behind the wainscot, but in point of intellect they are — there is only one word for it — "mutts."

As to a ghost story as an engine of terror under such circumstances, the mere idea becomes ludicrous. The modern guest in the East Wing would come calmly down to breakfast and say as he took his porridge — "There was an apparition in my room last night," in the same way that he would have spoken if there had been a bat in it. "Oh, I do hope it didn't disturb you?" says the hostess at the coffee pot. "Oh, not at all, I chased it out with a tennis racket." "Poor things," murmurs the lady, "but we don't like to get rid of them altogether. Teddy and Winifred are making a little collection of notes about them and their father's going to send it to the Psychical Research. But I do dislike the children sitting up at night in the ruined tower in the wood. It's so damp for them. Two lumps?"

So the ghost story is dead. Let it rest in peace — if it can.

Cross-Examining Santa Claus.

BY CHARLOTTE PERKINS GILMAN

From 'The Century' magazine, December 1922

ARE you a Christian — of any sort? Do you see Christmas (the Christ Mass) as a celebration of the birthday of Jesus? Are you interested in the pre-Christian origins of that celebration, in the long and swelling stream of pagan legend and primitive custom which had poured into that mid-winter festival before the Christian church adopted it?

Do you care for children not with shallow sentiment as something expected of every one, but with real affection? Do you love humanity, or perhaps wish to, and feel the beauty of trying even once a year to show that love? And what do you think of Santa Claus?

If your mind works clearly, you may well ask what the last question has to do with the others. And truly it has very little of a genuine nature. The invention of this bearded secular saint is only one tiny twisted twig on an enormous tree, if I may so mix my figures of speech. It is a comparatively recent growth, extremely local, in all ways negligible.

The beginning of the celebration is old indeed. It marks "the turn of the year," the winter solstice by the Julian calendar. The sun, visible fountain of life and comfort, health and pleasure, had been going farther and farther away, but paused for a little, and came back again. The day of that turning was a promise of joy, of spring and summer, of blossom and harvest.

Successive religions, each with its swirling cloud of myth and mystery, added continually to ancient habits, and the mid-winter festival spread far and wide, with varying attendant customs.

Through Rome, where the twenty-fifth of December was celebrated as the birthday of the unconquered sun, we trace back to the Syrian sun-god Baal; from Greece we get the worship of the child Dionysus, born of a maiden, near the same date; and in Mithraism, which ran neck and neck with Christianity for a time, sun-day was a holy day, dedicated to the sun.

It was natural enough that the early Christian fathers, struggling against the tide of pagan customs, should claim the day for the birth of their sun of righteousness.

If you are interested in the rich world of Christmas legend and custom, delve into "Christmas in Ritual and Tradition" by C.A. Miles. He shows how the Roman Saturnalia, just before Christmas, and the calends beginning on New Year's day, were times of joyous celebration, with kindness to the poor and to slaves, riotous jollification, banqueting, and drinking to excess; and how the early church, intensely ascetic, associating beauty, joy, and license with the heathenism they fought against, strove its best to turn the feast-day to a fast-day.

"The conflict was keen at first. The Church authorities fight tooth and nail against these relics of heathenism, these devilish rites; but mankind's instinctive paganism is insuppressible, the practices continue as ritual, though losing much of their meaning, and the Church, weary of denouncing, comes to wink at them, while the pagan joy in earthly life begins to color her own festival."

So followed the natural growth of Christian myth and custom, song and story, varying with race, country, and time; some still known to us, some left in the dark ages where they belonged, but under all is the beautiful truth taught by Him whose birth is commemorated.

§2

In no other religion has there been so lovely a vision as this, divine love coming on earth as a baby, a little child, that child growing up to teach of human unity, of God in man, of worship in love and service. It is more than fitting that such a birthday should come to be "the children's festival."

Every age has its preferred forms of expression, its specific customs, and Christmas, in social evolution, reflects the characteristics of every race and nation, every period, with its tastes and feelings. Throughout medieval Europe there survived many of the barbaric performances, dressing in skins and heads of beasts, or men in women's clothes; and much of the horrible remained also in hobgoblin, Ruprecht, and Klapperbock.

This Knecht Ruprecht, Klas, or Joseph went about with the procession of maskers, clad in skins in some regions, and gave the children nuts and apples if they could say their prayers perfectly; if not, he punished them. As Mr. Miles puts it, "In Protestant north Germany the Episcopal St. Nicholas and his Eve have been replaced by Christmas Eve and the Christ Child, while the name Klas has become attached to various unsaintly forms appearing at or shortly before Christmas."

St. Nicholas gradually became known as the children's patron saint, and "in the early seventeenth century a Protestant pastor is found complaining that parents put presents in their children's beds and tell them that St. Nicholas has brought them." This he said was "a bad custom, because it points children to the saint, whereas we know that not St. Nicholas but the holy Christ Child gives us all things for body and soul, and it is he alone whom we ought to call upon."

In this far-reaching work of Mr. Miles from which these quotations are taken, with its full bibliography, careful index, wealth of research, we find only one scant notice of our own pre-dominant "Saint": "As Santa Klaus St. Nicholas is of course known to every English child, but rather as a sort of incarnation of Christmas than as a saint with a day of his own. Santa Klaus probably has come to us via the United States, whither the Dutch took him, and where he still has immense popularity." In Dawson's "Christmas and Its Associations" he is mentioned only twice, giving the same origin.

This popularity, this supercession of all deeper, holier ideas and beliefs by a single fantastic superstition, is probably due to one misguided piece of verse.

"Let me make the songs of a people, and who will may make their laws," cried the wise man, or as Whitman the poet, "In war he is the best backer of the war — he fetches artillery as good as the engineer's — he can make every word he speaks draw

Dante showed us heaven and hell in vivid picture, Milton presented Satan as a tremendous personality, and the author of "The Night before Christmas" has given us Santa Claus, even to the names of his reindeers, with every detail of physical grossness, soot-soiled furs and stump of a pipe.

§3

Christmas has changed as we have changed, until today the prevalent idea of its celebration in our country, is roast turkey and a Christmas tree, a banquet and the giving and receiving of presents. With most Protestant Christians it is not so much a church festival as a family one, though even Unitarians sing "It came upon a midnight clear" and "O little town of Bethlehem" on the nearest Sunday.

The "Christmas spirit," however, is still urged, and we vaguely feel that this is something beyond the family circle. Special appeals for charity are made. Dinners are given to newsboys and other hungry persons. There is something pathetic, if not absurd, in the scant periodicity of our social affection, this loving one another in an annual spasm.

But for the most part Christmas is a domestic affair, and, as the children's festival, is in their minds almost wholly a matter of getting something good. Long before they are big enough to make their little gifts they have acquired the habit of receiving them. The most advanced illustration of this "Christmas spirit" is seen among crafty little boys who go to Sunday school assiduously in December, perhaps to more than one, with an eye single to the profits.

To what do we owe so sad and strange a collapse of our idealism? How has the birthday of the Child Jesus come to be an occasion for hypocrisy and greed in children, an opportunity for ingenious plans for self-aggrandizement?

Is it not visibly because of our substitution for the gracious and loving Teacher, the lover of all humanity, of this chimney-climbing distributer of presents, Santa Claus?

To what weakness in ourselves, what surrender to primitive relationships and minor gratifications, do we owe his looming so large as almost to obliterate the loveliest truth we know?

"St. Nicholas" is a dignified figure enough, but this most undignified "Santa"! It is one of the saddest descents in the history of mythology — Jesus, St. Nicholas, Santa Claus!

Look at the long story: first the legitimate celebration of a genuine god; then the wavering veils of custom covering the old beginnings; then the great new-seen truth set up on the old foundation, a nobler story than the sun-myths; then, gradually, new tales and customs obscuring the new truth, the saint instead of the deity; and at last, instead of the saint, this cheap fairy-tale of a red-nosed, pot-bellied, benevolent old kobold, who lies dormant up in the arctic regions somewhere from year's end to year's end, save for this one night's activity, this reindeer-and-sleigh affair, this bulging bundle, and chimney-sweep descent to distribute his benefactions.

A purely local legend, having no appeal in warm countries, with no element of beauty to make up for its lack of truth, the Santa Claus myth seems the poorest of all that have grown up in modem times around this ancient festival.

As first promulgated, we seem to find the coming of the saint as much of a threat as a promise, a sort of a parent's assistant; for the "good" child a present, for the "bad" one a birch rod, merely a part of the vain lying with which ignorant and incompetent parents have always tried to coerce their children.

There may be "truth" in fiction, "truth" even in fairy-tales, — many a wise myth or lovely legend has helped the human mind, — but there is also possible sheer degradation for old or young in unworthy fiction.

Then comes the outcry of sentiment, that superficial sentiment which attaches itself easily to whatever happens to be current, forgetting better things behind.

"Children love Santa Claus," we are told. To this we may answer that children above a certain age do not, for they know there isn't any such person; that children below a certain age do not, because they are too little for even fairy tales, and that those in between will soon outgrow their delusion. Then if no more of them are told the tale, they will miss nothing, for there are better ones.

But is it not a pity that we have roused that ineffably sweet and tender thing, the love of a child, and artificially attached it to this unworthy image?

Here is an annual rejoicing, represented to childish minds by glittering symbols and delightful toys and sweetmeats, a day kept because of the coming of the sun, and then of divine love in human form, and this golden opportunity to teach that divine love, to rouse returning love for human beings, which we deliberately divert to teach love for an empty fabrication.

Jesus said, "Suffer little children to come unto me," and we have driven them to Santa Claus instead!

His is an interested, even a sordid, affection. The real love making the gifts, the love of parents, brothers, sisters, friends, is not conditional. The mother often loves the "bad" child best, and the divine love we talk about was expressly directed to sinners rather than to the righteous.

Have we no foresight, no glimmer of knowledge of child psychology, that we dwell on the child's pleasure in believing the poor legend we teach him and forget his pain when he finds it false, that we have deliberately deceived him?

"I believed it long after the other children gave it up," says one. "I believed it because my mother told me it was so, and my mother never lied." What of her feelings when she found that her mother did?

Not all children suffer equally at this first great disillusionment; it depends on the intensity of their faith and love. Has not life enough of disappointment and loss that we should choose the first fresh years, the unquestioning faith of babyhood, to set up this cheap idol, which must so soon come down?

The child has no words to express a pain like this, the bitter, cureless grief of finding that what one loved is not, and never was. The shock of learning that the parents, the elders, those whom we wholly trusted, are not to be trusted; not merely that they may be mistaken, but that they tell what they know is false, this we prepare for our children. This we have given them in place of what we might have told, the historic legends which we may learn, the story of the religion which we believe, and our own real love, which we know.

We give them neither noble facts nor noble fancy. It is the ignobility of this petty myth which makes it undesirable even as a fairy-tale. The world is only slowly outgrowing its ancient weakness of superstition. There are still plenty of Christians who "knock on wood" without the faintest idea of why they do it, or any shame at doing a thing for which they have no reason.

One of our high race duties is to keep the minds of the new generations clear and strong in order that they may face the problems of their time more intelligently than we do ours. This does not cut them off from fairy-tale and legend, poetry and fiction. Imagination is one of our highest qualities, and needs more cultivation than it gets.

But the distinction between clear, beautiful, dependable truth and all the lovely play of fancy should be early learned. Life is full of pleasant and interesting truths of all kinds and sizes; a child may be led among them in wonderment and joy. They are eager for truth. To your best efforts they say, "Is it a true story?" The human soul, however young, wants truth. You can enjoy your "detective story" without believing it, and so can the child his fairy-tale, especially if his mind is enriched by early knowledge of strange things that are true.

"I pity the child who has no fairy tales," says one. Yes, but I pity the child to whom has not been opened the most marvelous, fascinating, and endless of fairy-tales — the book of life on earth. It is the poverty of our own knowledge, the sterile, mechanical education we have had, and our almost universal ignorance of child culture, which makes us capable of giving our children chaff instead of bread.

There are other results to consider besides the effect on the child mind. Because our thought of Jesus has been overlaid by the story of Santa Claus, our whole celebration has changed. Festivals of rejoicing, with dance and song, rich decoration and proud processional, may be overdone, deteriorate, and cheapen; but one, the main features of which are banqueting and exchanging presents, has an easy descent.

Because of this degradation of a once noble festival, we have fallen to such poor pretense that the humorist prays "Forgive us our Christmases as we forgive them who have Christmased against us!" Christmas means to us presents — presents rising in competitive expense; presents sinking in useless absurdity; presents the labor of selling which has made the blessed season a cumulative misery to those behind the counter, and such a tax and burden on those who buy that we see at last a healthy reaction in "The Society for the Prevention of Useless Giving" — the "Spug."

This giving of presents has small resemblance to the reverent tribute of the three kings of the East. It derives from pre-Christian sources, and, though ennobled by the giving love of Jesus, has been suffered to lapse again through letting that large love become obscured by intra-family exchange alone, and in the child's mind is based on a poor myth.

However based, it has grown, with our numerical and industrial development, into an annual economic frenzy — "the Christmas trade." To those who make and distribute things to sell not for any essential need, use, or beauty, but merely for sale, and to those who do the selling, who store, display, advertise, and hand over the counter, this ancient festival, joyous and holy, means that one thing, the Christmas trade.

Fancy celebrating the birth of Jesus by an orgy of commercialism!

It is this commercial Christmas which is now eagerly adopted by quite unchristian peoples, of any faith or no faith, with no mention or thought of Christ. It is no Christian occasion they are appropriating; it is merely a jollification, a gay holiday, a time for exchanging gifts.

There are some tender souls who cling to Santa Claus as something beautiful, and who talk of "the Christmas spirit" as if it emanated from that amiable hobgoblin. Yet Santa Claus has no basis but St. Nicholas, St. Nicholas none save in the Christian church, and the Christian church none save in Christ, from whom that Christmas spirit comes.

If we wish to keep up an ancient and legitimate festival of annual rejoicing merely as a race habit, there is no harm in that, — that would, of course, be open to any race, any religion, — but we should be honest about it and not call it "Christ mass."

If we are Christians, and keep the festival in honor of the founder of our religion, we assuredly should teach our children whose birthday we are celebrating, and why we try to show more love for one another on that day than is ordinarily convenient.

But neither an honest pagan nor an honest Christian need clog the growing mind with petty myths which they do not believe.

No one writer has done so much to deepen and widen the spirit of Christmas as Charles Dickens, humanitarian and child-lover that he was. But his well-known and well-loved collection of Christmas stories has no word about Santa Claus. The tree was there, — "that pretty German toy," he calls it, — and the last story in the book, "The Christmas Tree," has enough in it of shining beauty and pleasant gifts to satisfy any child's heart.

He goes back in memory to the Christmases of his own child-hood, reproducing those early impressions with a vividness which ought to teach the dullest of us to be careful what we give or allow to be given our children. The description of his baby terror at the Jack-in-the-box and other disagreeable objects, in especial the mask, a dreadful "false face," which haunted him in nightmares, ought to be an illumination to those who make and those who buy. Then, with "The Waits," he gives in lovely imagery the background of it all, the stories of the Holy Child of long ago.

Instead of memories of a misplaced love, a shattered faith, he looks back to this: "Encircled by the social thoughts of Christmas time still let the benignant figure of my childhood stand unchanged. In every cheerful image and suggestion that the season brings, may the bright star that rested on roof be the star to all the Christian world. ... This in commemoration of the law of love and kindness, mercy and compassion. This in remembrance of me."

Isn't that better than Santa Claus?

The Christmas Crèche and the Passion Play.

BY AMELIA VON ENDE

From "The Bookman" Magazine, December 1914

In her poetical play, *The Wolf of Gubbio*, Josephine Preston Peabody cleverly makes sue of the tradition which ascribes to St. Francis of Assisi the invention of the "crèche" set up in Catholic churches at Christmas. The village inn-keeper has set adrift a poor potter from a neighboring town, with wife and infant, because he expects a company of distinguished gentlemen pilgrims from France. The couple set out for the next town on foot, are attached by robbers. The husband is tossed over a cliff, the wife escapes with the loss of her purse, but cannot find the babe which she had hidden from the highwaymen. With some reluctance on account of its communistic features, the people of Gubbio prepare a Christmas feast; but the famous wolf, incensed at their cruelty toward him and one another, devours the contents of the kettle set up in the marketplace and disappears. The promise of a spread having vanished, St. Francis decides to treat them to a show, and curtaining off a part of the square, prepares a pictorial representation of the Nativity. The potter's wife who has been graciously given shelter in the tavern-stable, is to be the Virgin, the husband, who has been found by the French guests, Joseph, and in time the wolf brings in the lost baby. So the curtain descends upon a living picture of the Nativity of eloquent symbolism.

THE CHRISTMAS CRÈCHE

There is little doubt that the permanent plastic pictures of the Nativity owed their origin to the same religious and dramatic instinct which gave to us the Miracle and Mystery plays of the Middle Ages, and that their cradle was Italy. For the "crèche" was for several centuries so popular in that country that hosts of sculptors, woodcarvers and painters made their living by it. Nor was the art limited to representations of the Nativity. The Passion and other chapters of the New Testament were treated in the same manner. Crèche-craft developed into a legitimate branch of ecclesiastical art industry. No Christmas or Easter worship in churches, convents or the chapels of the wealthy and the noble was considered complete without a crèche. The crèches seen in most churches today give not the remotest idea of the art and the handicraft that went into the making of those plastic pictures. But a collection of specimens from the past makes one regret that the art is now to be reckoned among the lost arts.

Such a collection has been made by a citizen of Munich, Kommerzienrat Max Schmederer, and presented to the National Museum of his city. Realizing the value of the crèche as a religious and artistic manifestation of the past, he spent years in traveling and invested a fortune in collecting his treasures. He bought them from impoverished churches and convents or from private families in Italy, and Sicily, the Tyrol and Bavaria. He acquired not only complete crèches, but a large stock of individual figures and other objects need in their composition, and having entered deeply into the spirit of that art, he was able to set up besides the authentic crèches transplanted from their original sources a number of crèches of his own composition. They fill enormous glass cases in a special room of the Museum which he frequently visits and where he readily talks about them with the many native and foreign guests.

Among the Italian crèches in the collection one of the most admirable in composition, coloring and perspective is an "Adoration of the Shepherds," by Giovanni Matera, a sculptor of Palermo, who died in 1718. His figures are of terra cotta. An "Entombment" and "Descent

from the Cross," by Sammartino, another Neapolitan sculptor, who modeled his figures in clay, are full of life and feeling. Another Neapolitan artist, Savarino, was famous for his horses, which are a feature in a large circular crèche, representing "The Tent of the Three Kings,' which was originally in a palace in Naples. The house-crèche, however, was usually of small dimensions; one of the curiosities of the collection is a Sicilian house crèche with figures not more than three-fourths of an inch in size, set up in a Louis XV casket.

It is likely that Tyrolese and Bavarian artists studying in Italy were impressed with the artistic character and the commercial possibilities of this work and introduced it in their countries. For in the second half of the eighteenth and the first half of the nineteenth century Bavarian and Tyrolese churches and convents had some extraordinary crèches by men who were gradually identified with that work. One curiosity of the collection is a crèche made of parchment by Martin Kneller. Sebastian Habenschaden, a painter of old Munich, grateful remembered by his guild for the restaurant he founded in

the charming village of Pullach, was also a carver of crèches and excelled in animal figures.

The work of the Bavarian and Tyrolese artists is characterized by great simplicity and sincerity and by a realism which suggests their close connection with the people. The models were chosen from their immediate neighborhood and frequently represented with every detail of physical imperfection or disfigurement, a striking example being the figure of a woman with a goiter. The artists were of the people and knew that their art was of direct appeal to the people. The dramatic instinct is rather common in Southern Europe and especially in Austria and the Tyrol and the men and women who posed for the figures in these plastic pictures of the life of Christ entered as readily into the spirit of their parts as the actors of the Passion Play. A walk through the Schmederer collection makes one feel as if Oberammergau were but the dramatic realization of the large Passion crèche by Munich artists of the eighteenth century.

Not all the crèches in the collection have an indisputably correct setting. A very elaborate crèche from the Ursuline convent of Bozen, has a Tyrolese landscape as background of the manger. In Italian crèches the architecture is mostly of the Renaissance. Among the crèches made up by Herr Schmederer himself is one which was suggested by a passage in a letter of Goethe, dated May 27, 1787, in which the poet speaks of the crèches set up by the people of Naples on the roofs of their houses, with Vesuvius as the natural background. Herr Schmederer also reproduced "The Slaughter of the Innocents," from the painting of Lebrun. In all these arrangements the artist-collector has shown a rare feeling for line and color, symmetry and movement; they are animated stage pictures on a miniature scale.

A large part of the collection is devoted to crèches of a secular character. The art lent itself equally well to plastic representations of other subjects, and when the artists saw ignorant congregations trusting the work to the dilettantism of unskilled curates, they had to seek another outlet and market. Thus were composed elaborate scenes of the life and customs of the people which have an educational value as historical object lessons. One scene in the collection is delightfully characteristic of the Italian temperament: in front of a chapel with a diminutive crèche the people are engaged in dancing and merrymaking. There is an osteria with couples whirling about to the tune of bagpipes, fiddles and guitars; there is a market with butchers', bakers' and other booths, amply supplied with their wares and surrounded by a motley crowd of vendors and buyers. There are scenes from the life of the peasants and mountaineers.

Herr Schmederer has the true collector's sentiment: he handles his treasures with something like tenderness, for he respects the amount of religious sentiment and artistic aspiration that went into their making. Rare specimens of the extraordinary skill of workers in wood and metal, clay and terra cotta, who lived before our machine-made age, they appeal to people, like the Passion Play, regardless of creed.

A Christmas Pilgrimage.

BY ALLEN A. HUNTER

From "The Nation," December 27, 1922

It was Christmas morning. I was looking for the light of quiet healing, the brightness of good-will, that should usher in the friendly open hand in place of the old, clenched, shaken fist, for there had come upon me the memory of friends I would not see again, friends who had thrown away life in their faith that the nations would murder each other no more. So I went to the place where the Prince of Peace was born and watched the worshipers of clashing sects rattling their incense and reciting their prayers. But there was no healing, no brightness of good-will in the cave under the great Church of the Nativity

I walked up the twisting cobbled street, past a group of Bethlehem boys playing marbles — with dried figs — and came, half a mile fro the town of small white houses, to the field of the shepherds. I crossed the open space of barley stubble and stood beside the grove in the center, where they say the shepherds watched their flocks by night. I saw the "little gray leaves" of the olives twinkle and flash in a radiance of sunshine that smashed the clouds to pieces. A flock of goldfinches overhead were jubilant and generous with delicate bits of song. Yes, both heaven and nature sang. But neither had more to say than did the bleating sheep or the moss that clung to the ruined wall.

A CHRISTMAS PILGRIMAGE

Five miles back on the Arab pony to Jerusalem and St. George's. As I entered the cathedral door I said: "Here at least in this holy place (why, right over there through the window, is the little green hill of Calvary), here will 'shine the Infant Light.'" And to be sure, the vaults of the great church did ring and thrill as five hundred soldiers chorused "Hark the Herald Angels Sing." Those men stood stiff and true as they sang. They had fought a good fight. Every brass button, every inch of leather on Sam Browne belt and bandolier, every spur was polished and shining. There was, too, many a glorious ribbon above the heart that spoke of gallantry and valor. But I went away from that church unsatisfied still. They had knelt in awe and wonder. They had sung "Noël, Noël." The light of "a little stranger star" had shone upon them — for a passing moment. But would that light last? Would those men rise from their knees and go out from the holy place not only to hate the hideous waste of war, but to love the cause of peace, to love it with such a holy flaming passion as they had loved their country and their king?

There was no telling. I could only remember that those of us who feel we have the light of a new day in our eyes might never see that day. It might be that some of us would have to go down to another hell of burning bombs and shells, of bullets, of gas that twists the human face into inhuman shapes of agony, to the dreary, hopeless tedium of the trenches, and the mad resentment against the powers of this world.

Not too jubilant that Christmas morning, I returned to the orphanage up on the westernmost hill of Jerusalem, the orphanage that the American Red Cross had taken over a few months before from Pastor Schneller, the kindly, gray-haired German missionary who had given all he had to the fatherless children of Palestine. Here they were: hundreds of Syrian youngsters, mastering a trade in the apprentice shops, or learning to eat real food once more. It was dinner time. I went into the big orphanage kitchen to say Merry Christmas to Hilweh, the cook. She was active and smiling and radiant as always, and because this was Christmas Day she was wearing the steeple-like headdress of white muslin and the beautiful crimson and purple and blue embroidery on her breast that Bethlehem women wear. Hilweh seemed glad at her task, glad to be working as she stirred a huge wooden spoon in a brass pot. That mother of the strong arm and radiant face (she was mother to all the orphans, though she would have no fooling in her kitchen) was a Mohameddan, and too old, I suppose, to change her creed. Those whom she fed were oncoming Christian Armenians and Orthodox and Moslems who, if they had remained in their villages, would now be quarreling one with another, faith against faith, grudge against grudge. But here Mohammedan Hilweh doled out bread and lentils to Turk and Christian alike, and here this Christmas morning I found among her and her charges what elsewhere I had missed — Bethlehem.

The Country and Religion of the Magi.

BY A. HILLIARD ATTERIDGE

From "The Month" Magazine, January 1885

In one of the side chapels of the choir of Cologne stands the shrine of the Three Kings, probably the richest shrine in the Christian world, certainly the richest piece of medieval goldsmith's work that has escaped the pillage and destruction of the Reformation and the Revolution. The great Cathedral — the largest, and in the eyes of many the most splendid of Gothic Cathedrals — is itself, as it were, the outer case of this shrine. It was built to receive the relics of the Kings. Cologne is singularly rich in relics, what with the hundreds of skulls of the martyrs at St. Ursula's, St. Gereon's, and St. Maurice's, witnesses to the massacre of St. Ursula's virgins, and St. Maurice's Theban legionaries; but the treasure that did most to make Cologne a place of pilgrimage, and to win it its old title of *Heiliges Cöln*, was assuredly the shrine of the Kings. Their relics were brought to Cologne from Milan seven centuries ago, when the Kaiser Frederick Barbarossa, apparently regarding them as part of the spoil of the capture Lombard city, took them from the Church of San Eustorgio and gave them to his Chancellor Rainald, who was then Archbishop-Elect of Cologne. On July 23, 1164, Rainald deposited them in the old Cathedral. In 1337 they were placed in the chapel of the new choir, where they have lain ever since, except during the ten years at the end of the last century, when the costly shrine with its precious contents was removed from Cologne to save it from the destroying hands of the French invaders.

The history of the relics of the Kings is thus clear enough for seven centuries. We know how they came to Cologne, but it is not at all so clear how they came to Milan. More than one writer in modern books of reference, Catholic and non-Catholic, settles the question by stating that St. Eustorgius, Bishop of Milan, brought them from Constantinople. But this statement will not bear examination. It perhaps originated in the fact that the relics of the Kings were long honored in the Church of St. Eustorgius at Milan. There is, it is true, a medieval legend which describes in detail this translation of the relics of the Kings of Milan by the Saint, but the Bollandists attach no value to the legend, and point out that although we have in the works of St. Ambrose a eulogy of St. Eustorgius, to whose glorious memory he appeals, as to that of one of the most illustrious of his predecessors, he says not a word of this alleged translation of the relics of the Kings. The silence of Ambrose, especially when we consider his well-known devotion to the relics of the saints, is very strong evidence that these relics were not at Milan in his time — that is, at the end of the fourth century. They had certainly been at Milan for some centuries before their translation to Cologne in the twelfth — for local tradition appears to have connected them with St. Eustorgius, and this is enough to prove that at least they had not been brought very recently to Milan. The writer of the article on the Magi in Dr. Smith's *Dictionary of the Bible*, makes a statement on this subject which is clearly wrong; it would be interesting to know on what it is based. He tells us:

"Among other relics supplied to meet the demands of the market, which the devotion of Helena had created, the bodies of the Magi are discovered somewhere in the East, are brought to Constantinople, and placed in the great church, which as the Mosque of St. Sophia still bears in its name the witness of its original dedication to the Divine

Wisdom. The favor with which the people of Milan had received the Emperor's Prefect Eustorgius called for some special mark of favor, and on his consecration as bishop of that city, he obtained for it the privilege of being the resting-place of the precious relics.

Unfortunately for this story the hard facts of chronology are against it. The Church of St. Sophia was built by Justinian, who remained from 527 to 565. There were, as far as we can discover, only two prelates of the name of Eustorgius among the Bishops of Milan — one was St. Eustorgius, a predecessor of St. Ambrose; the other Eustorgius governed the see from 512 to 518; thus he was nine years dead before the builder of St. Sophia ascended the throne, and could not therefore have obtained any relics from the future church. So much for this story.

Still we can put nothing better in its place. This much is clear. The relics of the Kings were brought to Milan between the fifth and tenth centuries, a stormy time, when the record of such an event might well be lost, especially if, as may have been the case, they were first brought there in secret for security. There is an event in the subsequent history of the shrine which in this connection may explain the obscurity of the earlier history of the relics. In 1794, when the French Republican armies were advancing victoriously to the Rhine, plundering and destroying many a sanctuary in their Jacobin hate of holy things, the shrine of the Kings was secretly removed from the chapel, and carried off to Frankfort-on-Maine; even there it was not safe, and for some years it was moved from hiding-place to hiding-place in Southern Germany, its faithful guardians being at times reduced to such straits that they had to remove from the shrine some of the precious gems with which it is ornamented, and sell them to procure the necessaries of life. At length, after ten years of wandering, the shrine was brought back in safety to its chapel in the choir of Cologne on January 4, 1804. It may well be that the relics were first brought to Milan in secret to escape one of the destructive storms of the earlier Middle Ages, and it is quite possible the first left the East in the same way. It is difficult otherwise to explain the absence of documents bearing on this point. The suggestion that the relics were *"supplied* to meet the demands of the market which the devotion of Helena had created," or in other words, that they are suppositions, creates more difficulties than it solves, even from a purely historical point of view.

It is strange that just as so much obscurity hangs over the history of their relics, the history of the Magi themselves is also most obscure. We have only one trustworthy document bearing upon it, and that is St. Matthew's Gospel. It tells us only of their visit to Bethlehem. It tells us nothing of their previous history beyond what can be inferred fro the statement that they were — "wise men (Magi) from the East," and the narrative comes to an end (so far as they are concerned) with the statement that they return to their own country. Even its name is not given, and this is a point on which commentators on the Gospel are widely at variance. There are, however, two opinions, to one or other of which most of them give their adhesion — some make Persia the country of the Wise Men, others Arabia. The first opinion is supported by most of the monuments of early Christian art and by several of the earliest ecclesiastical writers; the second has in its favor the opinions of some of the early Fathers, and many later commentators, and, if I am not mistaken, it is the opinion most frequently adopted in modern Catholic works on the Gospels and the Life of our Lord.[1] This is not a little strange, for the evidence in favor of the second

---

1   Van Steenkiste, in his Commentarium in Matthaeum (1880), while adhering to the second opinion, thus sums up the patristic evidence for both views: "Unde venerunt? Ab orsente, ait M.; sed quaestio set quid per Orientem intelligendum sit. S. Chrys. Cum plerisque veteran (Clem. Alex. Strom. i. 15; S. Ephrem, De Maria et Magis; S. Bas., Hom. In Christ. generat. 5, ap. Migne, ili. 1470; S. Cyr. Alex. In Is. xlix. 12) intelligit Persidem, quae propria erat regio corum qui Magi olim vocabantur; alii Chaldaean seu Mesopotamiam designant; vix differt S. Leo (Serm. In Epiph.) qui dicit Magos venisse a remotissima Orientis parte. Sed probabiliot nobis videtur opinio Tert. (Adv. Jud. 9; Contra Marc. iii.13), S. Just. (Dial, cum Tryph. 78, 106), qui script in Palestina sec. ii. S. Epiph. (Expos. fid. 8), et ut videtur S. Amb. (In L. 2, doset Magos a Balaam genus duxisse), eos venisse ex Arabia, quod innuunt forum munera, quippe quae sunt fructus nativi Arabicae terrae. Eum autem Arabiae

view is by no means strong, and there is much more to be said for the first. I do not propose to fully review all the evidence for the two opinions here, but having touched briefly on the arguments usually adduced on both sides, I shall go a little more fully into a branch of the evidence for the first, or Persian theory, which it seems to me has not been given its full weight by Catholic writers on either side.

For the Arabian theory it is urged that (1) the gifts offered by the Kings were the products of Arabia — gold, frankincense, and myrrh; (2) that the Prophet foretold that "the Kings of the Arabs and of Saba would bring gifts,"[2] and the Church applies these words to the coming of the Magi in the Office of the feast; (3) that the expression, "the East," might well include the northern part of Arabia, stretching to the east of Palestine, the extent of the ancient Arabia being much wider than that which appears on modern maps; (4) that the fact of the Church having for so long kept the feast of the Epiphany only twelve days after Christmas is evidence of a tradition that the Kings arrived very soon after the Birth of our Lord — they could not possibly have come for Persia in that time, they might have come from Arabia; (5) finally, the authority of many of the early Fathers is alleged for Arabia.

Now let us take these arguments one by one, and see what can be urged against them and in favor of the Persian theory. Against the last it may be fairly argued that, so far as it proves anything, the testimony of the early Fathers is divided, and perhaps on the whole is more favorable to the Persian than the Arabian theory. As to the fourth argument, Father Coleridge has very well pointed out that the date of the feast proves very little as to the interval between our Lord's Birth and the coming of the Wise Men.

"From early times [he says] the feast of the Epiphany has been celebrated, as now, on the twelfth day after Christmas Day. This custom

---

tractum, qui ad Orientem Palaestinae situs est, cogitemus oportet." (In Matt. q. 65, vol. i., p. 101).

2 Psalm 71:10

fixes in our minds the idea that the visit of the Kings took place at a like interval of time after our Lord's actual Birth, and thus before the Purification. But it is far from certain that the dates at which the great mysteries of our Lord are usually celebrated, were originally fixed, in all cases, on account of any very constant tradition. Again, even if this were the case, the date so fixed would only signify the anniversary of the mystery celebrated on a particular day. It would not of necessity fix the distance in point of time between one actually occurrence and another. If the visit of the Kings were a year and twelve days after the Nativity, its anniversary would be on the same day as if the interval were either twelve days only, or two years and twelve days. The longer intervals here named are more in accordance with the Sacred Test than the shortest of the three. It is certain that St. Matthew tells us that Herod diligently inquired as to the time of the appearance of the star, and that when he afterwards ordered the massacre of all children "from two years old and under," the limits of age was fixed in consequence of the information which the Kings had given. It is therefore natural to suppose that the star had been seen a year and some months before the Epiphany.[3]

He has further shown that grave harmonistic difficulties disappear if we take the longer interval. We may therefore conclude that the fourth argument proves nothing against the Persian theory, while the indications of the longer period in St. Matthew are decidedly in favor of it.

The third argument which explains the East to mean Northern Arabia, is less a new proof, than an attempt to meet an obvious difficulty. St. Matthew's words apply much more naturally to Persia. So we have Prudentius singing how "in the heart of Persia's realm where the sun starts upon his course," the Magi recognize the standard of the King:

> En Persici ex orbi sino,
> Sol unde sumit januam,

---

3   'Life of our Life,' vol. i., pp. 58, 59.

Cernunt periti interpretes
Regale vexillum Magi.

Nor does the second argument, from the words of Psalm 71, prove anything against the Persian theory. The Psalmist sings of the glories of the reign of Solomon, but it is of Solomon as the type of the future Prince of Peace, and so his words are such as could not apply merely to even this the most powerful of the Jewish Kings. The future Ruler is to reign through all generations, and His shall be a worldwide empire:

> He shall rule from sea to sea,
> And from the river unto the ends of the earth,
> Before Him the Ethiopians shall fall down,
> And His enemies shall lick the earth.
> The Kings of Tharsis and the island shall offer presents,
> The Kings of the Arabians and of Saba shall bring gifts,
> And all the kings of the earth shall adore Him,
> All nations shall serve Him.[4]

Even commentators who on other grounds favor the Arabian theory, reject this argument, pointing out that the prophecy is not of the coming of the Magi, but of the vocation of the Gentiles, of whom they were the first-fruits — thus it does not even prove that they were Kings. If it were a distinct prophecy of their coming, how is it that St. Matthew, who is continually pointing out the fulfillment of prophecy, makes no reference to it?

Finally, to the argument that they offered the products of Arabia as gifts, the ready reply is that their offerings were such as might have been easily obtained in any Eastern land. We even find St. Ephrem, who lived and wrote in Syria, speaking of them as the products of Persia, in his poem on the Wise Men. "Joyfully," he says, "the Persian princes took the gifts belonging to their land, and brought to the Virgin's Son gold, myrrh, and frankincense."

We thus see that some of the arguments adduced in favor of the Arabian theory prove little or nothing, while others apply equally well,

---

4   Psalm 71:8-11

or even better, to Persia. It is also to be noted that a strong traditional argument in favor of Persia is afforded by the monuments of early Christian art. The visit of the Magi, the first-fruits of the Gentiles, was naturally a favorite subject with the artists of the catacombs and the early basilicas, and in these pictures we find almost invariably the three Wise Men clad in a distinctly Persian dress.

But just as the central argument for the Arabian theory really is the supposed fulfillment in the visit of the Wise Men of the prophecy about the Kings of the Arabs and of Saba, so the chief argument for the Persian theory really centers upon the title given to the Wise Men by St. Matthew. He calls them "Magi from the East," and the argument rests upon what is implied by this. The Magi were the learned and priestly class of religion of ancient Persia. It is true that at the time when the Gospels were written, the word Magus was used a little loosely in its secondary sense of "Magician.' We have an instance of this in the title given to the Samaritan, Simon Magus, in the Acts of the Apostles. But this fact, though it diminishes the force of the proof, and prevents it from being absolutely demonstrative, is very far from destroying it, especially if we take into account other considerations pointing to Persia. This much the use of the word Magi by St. Matthew does absolutely prove — that the Wise Men were either of the priestly Magian class of Media and Persia (which then formed portions of the Parthian Empire), or that they were in some sense magicians. Now, let us see which of these interpretations is the more probable.

St. Thomas, in that part of the *Summa* which deals with the mysteries of our Lord's life, examines the question, "Whether those to whom the Birth of Christ was made manifest were befittingly chosen?"[5] He suggests the difficulty that it would seem to be most fitting that Divine Truth should be made manifest to the friends of God. "But the Magi appear to have been God's enemies, for we read in Leviticus 19, 'Go not aside after wizards, neither ask anything of soothsayers.'"[6]

---

5   'Summa Theologiae, iii. q. 36, a. 3.

6   V. 31, where the Vulgate has "Magos."

But he replies to the difficulty in the words of St. Augustine: "Even as ignorance prevailed in the rustic simplicity of the shepherds, so impiety prevailed in the sacrilegious rites of the Magi; nevertheless He who is the Corner-stone attracted both to Himself, inasmuch as He came to choose the foolish things in order to confound the wise; and not to call the just, but sinners; so that no one who is great may be proud thereof, and that no one who is weak may despair."[7] And then St. Thomas adds: "But some say that these Magi were not wizards, but learned astronomers, who were called *Magi* among the Persians and Chaldeans."

Now it is to be remarked that if the lesson which St. Augustine drew from the choice of the Magi to be among the first adorers of the newborn King is the true one, it is very strange that Scripture gives not the slightest indication that the Magi either had been in any notorious way sinners, or were now penitents. And if we may venture to answer St. Thomas' question, surely it does seem far more befitting that those who were the first-fruits of the Gentiles, the first adorers of the Holy Child, who came from beyond the limits of the chosen people, should be men who had kept the natural law, and could be called good and just, men such as, we may believe, God's providence has in all times raised up even among pagan peoples, such men as are usually among the first converts when the Gospel is at length preached to their people. The other alternative is, that the Kings were "magicians;" in that case they were one of two things, either men who had real commerce with the demon, or men who were impostors and pretended to possess an occult knowledge, while they were really mere charlatans. Surely it does not seem likely that such would be chosen out of all the Gentile world for this most exceptional grace. It is of course possible, but is it probable, that such was the case, especially when hey are in no way explicitly represented to us as penitents, any more than the simple shepherds, or Simon and Anna the prophetess?

---

7 Serm. de Epiph.

On the other hand, if ambassadors were to be chosen out of the Gentile world to lay their homage at the feet of the Messias, it would seem most befitting that they should be chosen from among the followers of one of the higher forms of Gentile religion, worshippers, if such there were, of one God. Such were the Persian Magi, and it may be added that they had at various times just those close relations with Judaism that seem to be implied in the language of the Wise Men.

The religion of the Magi was the so-called Zoroastrian or Mazdean religion. It was certainly the religion of the Persian Empire under the later Achaemenid Kings. The Greek conquest under Alexander, and the rule of the Greek Sovereigns of the house of Seleucus inflicted a severe blow upon the professors of Zoroastrianism; but when the Graeco-Persian gave way to the Parthian Empire, and again a purely Asiatic dynasty ruled from the Euphrates to the Indian frontier, the Magi began rapidly to rise in power and influence, until at last, in the third century after Christ, they were strong enough to place one of their number, the Magian Ardeshir (Artaxerxes), on the throne, and inaugurated the new Persian Empire of the Sasaanidae, of which the religion of Zoroaster was the very life and soul. The Birth of our Lord occurred in the transition period, when the Magi were rapidly rising to power and influence in the Parthian Empire, and when their religion, though not that of the State, was still widely spread throughout the populations that were under its rule.

We know what this Magian and Zoroastrian religion was, not merely from the fragmentary notices of classical and early Christian writers, but from its sacred books, preserved with religious care among the Parsis, who are no other than the descendants of these Persians, who are no other than the descendants of these Persians, who, on the conquest of their country by the Mohammedans, took refuge in India rather than abandon the religion of their fathers. The oldest portion of the sacred literature of Parsiism is a book, or rather a collection of books known as the Avesta (or, less correctly, Zendavesta). Written in an old Persian dialect that had ceased to be a living language, at or soon after the Christian era, it is certainly, as a whole, older than the time of our Lord, and thus, if the Magi of St. Matthew were Persians, we can read in the Avesta some of the same religious lore in which they were trained. The book is a collection of laws, traditional legends and formulas and hymns of praise. There is as yet no complete version by any English scholar,[8] and some of the incomplete versions published in England are on many grounds not to be recommended. In the languages of the Continent there are two masterly versions, the German version of Professor Spiegel, and still more recent the French version of Professor de Harlez, of Louvain. This last, with its elaborate introduction and notes, is, perhaps, at this moment the best existing summary of all the results of modern research into the religion of Zoroaster.

That religion was like all Pagan religions, a very imperfect one, and in its Bible — or rather, Book of Law and Ritual — the Avesta, there is much that is puerile, not a little that is repulsive; but at the same time there are certain features in it which, with all its defects, place it on a much higher standards than the other Gentile religions of antiquity.

Some portions of the Avesta are more or less clearly monotheistic in character. In the greater part of it, dualism, the conflict of two eternal powers of evil and of good, is the leading feature, and at times minor genii of good and evil become so prominent, that it is easy to see polytheistic tendencies at work. This mingling of various elements in the same book and the same religions has been variously explained. Some see in it the evidence of a progress from lower go higher forms of thought: others again the gradual decay of a purer faith; others — and this seems the most probable theory — look on this as evidence that the religion of the Magi was the outcome of contact with various forms of religious thought from monotheism downwards. But these are questions that cannot be discussed here. Whatever was

---

8 We can hardly count as such Bleck's translation of Spiegel's version, made for the use of the Parsis.

the origin of Zoroastrianism, its God, Ahura Mazda (*i.e.*, the All-Wise Lord), the Ormuzd of later writers, is a glorious conception, whether he appears in solitary grandeur as the all-pure and almighty creator of all things, or as the creator of the world of good, the revealer of the holy law, the eternal enemy of Angra-mainyus (Ahriman) and all his evil realm. His very names, "the Lord, the Wise One, the Disposer of all things, the Creator, He who counts up merit, He who saves," recall the attributes of the true God.

The central idea of the whole system of the Avesta, and the religion it teaches, is that of the strife between good and evil. The Avestic idea of evil is indeed a false one. The old teachers of the Holy Law of Zoroaster had not grasped the idea, that even as darkness is not anything existing as a positive reality, but is only the absence of light, so evil is essentially negative, a falling away form, a loss or privation of the full completeness of being, which we call good. Evil was for them the positive creation of a being of evil nature, not a fallen angel, but one who had always been evil, *Angramainyus*, the "evil-minded one," whose name is more familiar to us in its later contracted from of Ahriman. On the other hand, *asha*, or purity, is what makes the professor of the Holy Law just, and worthy of Paradise, the *ashavan*, or possessor of *asha*, is the righteous man. He does not posses it by mere ceremonial purity, though he can lose it by a neglect of legal prescriptions on this point. The *ashavan* is not the mere exact observer of ceremonies, but he is also the man "of good thoughts, good words, and good deeds" (*humata, hûkhta, huvarsta*), and this formula recurs again and again in the Avesta.[9]

Thus there was in the religion of the Magi the worship of one spiritual supreme God, and a central idea of the nature of moral goodness, which was a very exalted one. For the Magian as for the Jew idolatry was an apostasy. The Magian like the Jew had a complex ceremonial

---

9   A complete refutation of the theory held by M. Darmesteter and others, that 'asha' meant only the exact performance of external ritual, will be found in Professor de Harlez's 'Origins de Zoroastrianisme.'

law beside the moral law, and closely linked with it. But what is more, the Magian like the Jew looked for the coming of a future deliverer.

In the Avesta the power of Ahriman is not to last forever. Continually opposed and kept in check by Ahura and his righteous servants, his empire is to be at length destroyed. One of the legends contained in the Vendidâd, the ceremonial portion of the Avesta, describes Zoroaster in conflict with the demons of Ahriman, who strive to slay him. He drives them off by repeating a sacred formula in praise of all the good creation of Ahura, and then predicts their ruin, at the coming of "Saoshyant, the conqueror of demons." The name Saoshyant is a participial form, and means giving help, or favors; the Gracious, or the Helpful, would perhaps represent it in English.

We hear of Saoshyant again in one of the concluding prayers of the Yasna, or sacrificial liturgy of the Avesta. The prayer invokes in succession all the Fravashis, or guardian genii of the good creation, and concludes:

> We honor the Fravashis of righteous men,
> We honor the Fravashis of righteous women,
> And all the good, strong, and pure Fravashis of the righteous,
> From Gâyo Meretan even to the victorious Saoshyant.

That is to say, of all the righteous from the first man to Saoshyant, who, as we shall presently see, is to come at the end of time. The same expression is repeated in another prayer, where we hear again of all the good and holy "from Gâyo Meretan to Saoshyant the conqueror."

In another portion of the Avesta, in one of the Yashts or hymns, we find Saoshyant spoken of in connection with the Zoroastrian doctrine of a future restoration of all things. The hymn, after praising in turn the Fravashis of all just men, comes at length to Saoshyant, and continues thus:

"We honor the Fravashi of the pure Astvatereta [*i.e.* literally he who succors, he who raises up, corporeal beings], whose name shall be Saoshyant the victorious; whose name shall be Astvatereta. He is Saoshyant, in that he will favor all the visible world, he is Astvaterera, in that being endowed with a body and a vital principle, he will stop the destroyer of created beings, he will stop the demon (druj), he will stop the hate of the destroyer of purity."

Still more distinctly in another of these hymns Saoshyant is described as he who will make all things new and bring about the final resurrection of the dead. The hymn celebrates in turn the glory of each of the heroes and good genii of the Zoroastrian religion, and comes at length to Saoshyant, of whom it says:

"We honor that mighty royal splendor which belongs to Saoshyant, that he may renew the world, making it exempt from age and death, exempt from corruption and decay, always full of life and prosperity, directed according to his will — so that the dead shall rise, and the immortality of living beings shall come to pass; he effects the renewal of being, even as he desires. We honor this terrible kingly splendor: that Astvatereta [*i.e.* The raiser up of corporeal beings = Saoshyant] may come from the Kansu sea — he the minister of Ahura, the son of Vispataurvairi, full of knowledge, he who shall bring the final victory. ... He will see with the eyes of wisdom all creatures, he will strike the demon Paesis, he will look upon all the created world with eyes whose glance produces prosperity. He will finally establish the created world in the state of immortality.

"Behold the comrades of Astvatereta advance, of that Astvatereta who is holy in thought, in word, in deed, holy in nature: they speak no lying word, their tongue is mistress of itself."

Then the poet tells how the demons will fall down before their conqueror, "and Ahriman, the contriver of evil deeds, will bow down vanquished, stripped of all his might."

Though it is not distinctly stated in the Avesta, there is at least one clear allusion to the tradition that the future deliverer was to be born of a virgin mother. Moreover, in the Bundahîsh, Saoshyant appears as the Judge of the world in the Final Judgment, but it is right to add that this book is probably more recent than the Christian Era, and some portions of it may have been influenced by Christian teaching.

But in the passages we have cited from the Avesta there is evidence enough of the hope of the followers of Zoroaster in a future deliverer. Now the Jewish captivity produced a very close contact between the peoples beyond the Euphrates and the sons of Israel, tens of thousands of whom never returned to Palestine, but remained settled in the lands to which their fathers had been forcibly transferred. The Magi had therefore opportunity enough for becoming acquainted with the fact that the Jews too were looking for a future deliverer, who was to conquer all evil and change the face of the earth. The contact between the professors of the two religions of the Avesta and of the Old Testament is certain from history, and so many are the points of contact between them that while rationalistic commentators have insisted that many points in Jewish and Christian doctrine are really derived from the Avesta, Catholic writers have not denied the points of resemblance, but have replied that if there was any borrowing the Magi borrowed from the Jews. This second view is now made very probable by the comparatively late date which recent research is more and more clearly assigning to the Avesta. The fact of contact is, however, too clear to be denied, however it may be explained.

If, then, we suppose the Magi of St. Matthew to have been men of the priestly class from Persia, that is from the Parthian Empire, we may well suppose they were among the best of their class, men who clung to what was highest in the religion of their fathers, worshippers of one God, men who held that holiness lay not merely in outer form, but also in purity of word and thought and deed, men too who expected the coming of a future conqueror of evil, and knew from the sons of the Jewish exiles something of the hopes of Israel. They would thus be sharers in that general expectation which Tacitus and Suetonius tell us had spread through the East, that Asia was to gather new life and strength from some great change in which Judaea was to play a leading part. We can well understand how the minds of such men would be ready to welcome the Divine message that told them of the realization of their hopes, though in a way so different from all that mere human foresight would expect. This is certainly a more probable view than the curious theory of some commentators that the Wise Men were sprung from Balaam's people, and knew of his prophecy by tradition!

All this bears upon the question with which the second part of this inquiry began; it will be seen that the argument that the Magi of St. Matthew were from Persia, and not wizards from Arabia, is greatly strengthened by what we have learned in recent years of certain features of the old faith of the Avesta. But still it must be confessed that the theory that the Magi came from Persia is not certain, but at most very probable. It would seem that the obscurity in which the Scriptures have left the personality of the Magi will never be cleared up. At most we can but clear away the further obscurity caused by baseless traditions that make them kings and fix on them imaginary names.

In St. Ephrem's beautiful poem on the coming of the Magi, our Blessed Lady bids them farewell with the words, "May Persia rejoice at your message, and Assyria exult at your return; and when the Kingdom of my Son shall be made manifest, He shall plant His standard in your land." We may feel quite sure that the Christian poet's instinct speaks here aright, that the Savior who drew the Magi to His feet did not allow them to fall back into Gentile darkness, but that there was a connection between their return to their own land and the early progress of Christianity beyond the Euphrates, even tough we know nothing of their personal share in it. Later on, under the persecution of Shâpur, Persia gave hosts of heroic martyrs to the Church, but despite these persecutions and the subsequent Mohammedan conquest, the faith has never wholly disappeared from the land of the Magi. The standard of the Babe of Bethlehem has remained planted in their land, even though the army mustered under it is but a small one. Will the day eve come when the faith in the redemption of which the Wise Men were the first-fruits among the Gentiles will have won Persia and the ancient East to itself, and pilgrims from distant Asia will find their way to the shrine where the relics of those first pilgrims of the East rest in the choir of Cologne?

Christmas at Pont-à-Mousson.

BY EMORY POTTLE

From 'The Century Magazine,' December 1917

I PICKED it up this morning — my diary *en campagne* — from a dusty heap of papers, a little, ugly, squarish, black, stained book, scrawled through with faded inkings. Clasped about its middle is a thick, rough-edged rubber band. The original purpose of that was to hold in place the folds of a new pink inner tube. I remember the day I put them on — the tube and the band. Coming home from a soldiers' *fête* it was, one night in December — the 346th's. They were *en repos* at Dieulouard, and had organized a vivacious evening of vaudeville — the jokes were "thick," oh, very! — in a barn. T— and I, passing in our ambulance, heard the joyful roar and stopped in. *"Voilà les Américains!"* roared the *poilus*, vociferously hospitable. Section II — ours — was a favorite with 346. For months we had carried them dead and alive and wounded and dying. But if they loved us, we loved them more. That night they would have it that we oblige with a "turn." So we took the stage brazenly and bawled "Tipperary" to a thousand of them, in a fog of cheap tobacco smoke and such a rich human stench as you've never met unless you've been out there yourself. They gave us fulsome applause, but afterward I found out incidentally that the popular impression had been that *ces messieurs les Américains* were going to do a "jeeg" (very soft j). There was in consequence some mild regret at our inability to jig it.

Coming back that night, the long, low reaches of flat land, moonstruck, as white as death, icy, austere, with the Moselle like a shining shroud, were strangely beautiful — beautiful and alien, and as terrible as the gates of death itself. And death was very near us there always.

We had a bursted tire to replace that night, a new inner tube. Its confining elastic was snapped around my diary, which by chance bulged in my tunic pocket. There's the connection. And here I am back again to the little, ugly, black book, which I picked up this morning for the first time in many months. Quite oblivious, I have sat reading it a long, long time. The Great War; and I, a sharer, unknown, unnoted, negligible, but yet a sharer; France; her battlefields; her splendid dead; her splendid living; my part of it; to be a part of it again; my little life there — all this feels yet so big, so amazing, so fantastic to me. A whole world gone mad; lives broken to bits and fashioned again; confusion; destruction; desperation; death; and somehow victory — fragments such as these were in my head, in my heart, as I read the little book. The crowded, crashing streets of this tumultuous city are forgotten; forgotten the traffickings and strifes, the sharpnesses of life and the sweetnesses of love, cares and comforts, and dear securities. Once again I am out there in the gray and the filth and the mud and the horror and the suffering and the death of it. And, oh, strange vagary of mind! it seems, that hell of man's world, the more real thing.

It is incongruously enough some thought of Christmas, I believe, which has led me to hunt out the diary, some notion of recalling what I might have wonderingly made out of that gentle season at Pont-à-Mousson — my first war Christmas in France. For those faded scrawls have a sense now, I surmise, little guessed as I set them briefly down, cold and stiff of finger, in comfortless, unoccupied moments, waiting as the "next out," or huddled in some desolate *poste de secours* till my wounded were brought in from the trenches.

There is a note — December 7 — that my eye falls upon as I retrace the days of that month in an effort to discover whatever signposts of Christmas-time I might have set up. "It is the moment to write Christmas letters to be carried home by W—, who is leaving. Peace on earth, good will to men is about as congruous here," I wrote, "as would be the appearance in the Glycine of the Lord Christ Himself."

The Glycine — flowerful appellation — was the name, let me add, of the villa in which our section was quartered, unmercifully modern, new, artfully hideous. It was battered and scarred and dreary and debauched, but its roof was still holeless, and some of its broken panes we had replaced with oiled-silk. Entering at the basement through a bulky hedge of sandbags, past the one-time laundry, where were the telephones and the sallow-faced, despondent young French operator, and up a villainous flight of stairs, you found yourself in the *clou* of the establishment, *salle à manger, salle de lecture, salle de recreation*, whichever you liked. It was a high, humorless, vicious room, painted in the cheery tone of dried blood. There were a vast, slipshod, oval table, a feeble little stove (labeled misleadingly a salamander), some chairs, portions of a plaster-of-Paris gentleman indelicately attired, a muddy heap of ill-smelling garments — ours — in a corner.

W— was going home, starting tomorrow. A dozen of us bent over the big table, and scribbled letters he was to take in his pockets to mail in New York. It seemed rather unbelievable. We were writing, I suppose, to the few whom we best loved, who loved us best, saying cheerful Christmasy things to allay unallayable fears and anxieties. There we were, an obstreperous little republic washed up on the bleak shores of battle, come for various reasons, no doubt; but, clouded or unclouded, I think there was in every stirred heart an ideal, a beautiful one — France, home, Christmas. The pens scratched. Someone idly wrenched godless ragtime from the petulant piano we had filched from a deserted house. One lost oneself in gentle thoughts of those who would eagerly break the seals of the war-worn letters, and in their thoughts; lost oneself, and roused, with the journeying mind's instant of blurred hesitation, to the familiar racket out there, a mile away, sounds like the far slamming of great metallic doors. "It's an *arrivée*," or, "It's a *départ*," the wise ones would murmur.

The whole curious assortment of us drivers, disparate, various, as odd-shaped as pieces of a sawed puzzle, how closely we were drawn together, how affectionately bound, how amazingly fitted one to another to make out that picture "at the front!" Perhaps it was the common danger, always flapping black-winged over our little world, the common loneliness, unvoiced; perhaps it was some dread of death that interlaced our affections. But I like to think it was something rarer, finer, than these. That night, when the letters were written, we talked, I remember, a long time about home, and the voices were very gentle and subdued. I suppose we were wondering whether we should ever again go home — home to Christmas. Some of that night's group lie now in the rich-stained soil of France. Only their spirits, "radiant evermore," will come transfigured back. Their lives were laid down, in Eliot's rich phrase, as debonairly as a lover casts a rose at the feet of his mistress.

It is strange that war should bring out of a man with his pals all that is sweetest and deepest and kindest in him. Yet it is true that it does, though that night, I must confess, we were vaguely, good-naturedly a little envious, a little resentful of W—, who was going home for Christmas.

It was on the eleventh of December, it appears, that I went for the first time to Nancy, twenty kilometers away. There was much ado over obtaining the *laissez-passer*, much showing of it to prying bridge sentries. "A tidy place," I wrote down, "giving the impression of having been built on a large scale out of children's blocks for their diversion. The feel of a city was good after weeks of these foul, black, wretched, mud-plastered villages. Coming back here there were clear bits of glowing sky above blue-purple hills, reflected again in the overflowing Moselle, lying like a marsh-lake in its valley."

Oh, it was disconcerting — Nancy — that day, bewildering, with us in our soiled, worn uniforms come dripping, so to speak, out of the war-tide; and the Nanciens, the brightly clad officers in town dress, striding in and out of cafes and restaurants and shops; and women, — Oh, marvel of God's handiwork! — pretty women, officers' wives, sweethearts, maybe. How we stared! There was a huge bazaar that seemed to hold every buyable thing. And the incredible Christmas gifts! It was filled, in pleasant holiday movement, with women who led by the hand children. Toys there were, and boxes of sweets. I bought, I recall, a rich-looking bottle of very sweet champagne for Colonel B—, fat, brusk, eye-twinkling old B—, who 'd delightfully befriended me ever since the day his pet sergeant had been horribly wounded, and I had hauled him off in my ambulance to the surgery in time to save his life. That and a box of cigars for the three jolly *blageurs* who spent their lives at the telephones in the "Trench Central" at Monteauville were my only Christmas oblations. Yet on the way back to the City of Dreadful Night (so I thought of Pont-à-Mousson) I was aware of wishing I had not gone to Nancy. That bright glimpse of coming Christmas, men and women in what seemed then such a glow of security, and for us the gashed, gouged roads, the fast-falling night, and worse! But the clear sky and the purpling hills were beautiful, fantastically so, in a world that was grimmer and uglier than I had dreamed a world could become.

Yet observe now the vagaries of war and the futility of deductions: the first day of January the Germans with their great guns shelled that toy-city of Nancy, tore it and twisted it, martyred it and murdered it. By an odd chance I entered the place an hour or two after the bombardment. It was shut and sinister. Death shivered in the pretty streets. Emptiness and fear took tangible shapes. The bazaar was in ruins. At a little station on the edge of the town all those women, lately so charmingly clustered over Christmas counters, were standing, hundreds of them, in the rain, their possessions absurdly huddled at their feet, all stricken and frightened and desperately struggling for flight. I was glad, then, that they had struck their slender note of Christmas undismayed.

CHRISTMAS AT PONT-À-MOUSSON

One day a week was one's own — *repos. Ráy-po* was the section's pronunciation. One of those freedoms fell for me on the thirteenth. It is a very vivid memory, that day, even now. On it I came nearer to death than I have ever been, and I bought some hand-painted Christmas cards. It was this way, just as I set it down that night, afterward:

"Toward ten — a fine, fair morning, with melting snow — I walked up to Clos Bois (an evil little first-aid post in a horrible wood a mile above us), struck down into a narrow, woody gorge and across a brook, then up a hillside through a sparse forest that thickened ultimately into the fateful Bois le Prêtre — the Priest's Wood. Along rough tracks, knee-deep at times in an ooze of mud, I was going to find my friend Jennat, the captain, stationed in a sector called the Quart en Réserve. It was very lonely, the walk; rather frightening, too. I never met a soul along the cart-track. The wood was sinister, murderous. Many trees were cut, hundreds of others cruelly torn and splintered and lacerated by Boche shells. Over my head sounded the beat of the air-planes, like the ripping of silk high in the air, with the occasional whine of shrapnel tearing over the valley to the French batteries opposite. At the top of the long rise — nothing welcomer — I ran into lazy groups of artillerymen, who sent me on my complicated way to the captain's quarters. They were dug into the side of a hollow where the land dipped just on the edge of the third line, and down a flight of steps covered with tree-trunks, sandbags, sods, tarpaulins.

"Jennat was on his morning round in the first line, so I sat and talked an hour with a fat, lank-haired Basque doctor. He told me a strange story. It happened one morning after the Boches had been driven back into the wood. He was walking near a tree on the branches of which hung something he could not name. He took sticks and stones and dislodged it. It fell at his feet — a human heart, a naked human heart! It had been lodged there by some trick of cannon-play in a tree in the wake of battle. As he dryly told the story, it seemed to me very beautiful and terrible, a sort of holy symbol of the grief and glory of France. I wish I were a poet great enough to put that symbol into words; but I cannot.

"Jennat (we became acquainted over the dead body of one of his lieutenants weeks ago) appearing in great good humor, he and I and his officers sat down to lunch in another cave-room, at a table covered with red and green linoleum. There was yellow oiled-silk (like sunlight) at the windows, a fire in the stove, a basket with a cat and four foolishly new kittens. The lunch was remarkably good. They were a jolly lot, and very hospitable to *l'Américain*. We ate in an ungodly roar of mine-fire — from the Germans. Afterward Jennat took me into the first lines. There was. Water always over our ankles, often knee-deep, in the trenches. Engineers, wet to the waist, were trying to canal the water into the trenches but little used. They blagué-ed one another good-humoredly despite their plight. Splendid chaps all of them. At last we emerged into the first line. I was speaking very low, it seemed to me, but suddenly Jennat put his fingers to his lips, saying, 'S-s-s! *Il est là!*' I stared stupidly through a loophole in the sandbags — stared and started back. *He was there*, forty feet away, perhaps — *the Boche!* Theirs was a little' line, like ours, among the shattered trees. They must have heard our voices, for as we stood motionless, my eye caught a little cloud of black overhead. Then came an explosion, a crash, the sound of splintering wood, with bark in our eyes. The grenade had hit the trunk of a tree just outside the parapet, directly in line with us. Without that tree—

"'*Planquez-vous!*' Jennat cried. And that is roughly, 'Plank yourself!' I stood, quite unafraid, in amazement. He said it again peremptorily, pointing to a small cave. I obeyed. Crawled into the *boyau* meanly, huddled there abject and — well, I may as well be honest — cursed with a kind of physical fear the like of which I'd never dreamed of. Out on my feet, in the open, I was indifferent; but here! And there, beside me, cross-legged on wet straw, serene, I discovered a young soldier very delicately and dexterously painting bouquets of flowers and Christmas sentiments on postcards!

"I think a dozen grenades fell, harmlessly, it turned out. And at last I was free. I bought a handful of the painted cards from that remarkable young man. One of them I shall always keep. *'Bonnes fêtes,'* it simperingly says, beneath a bunch of marguerites. Sardonic suggestion! But I believe God suffers, too, with all the suffering of His poor, little bewildered children.

"I came home out of the dreadful wood and down by the soldiers' burial ground, which encroaches daily on the empty spaces of the grim hillside. There is a granite column under some leprous pines at a crossroad. It bears a wrought iron cross. One reads in discolored letters that 'God so loved the world — ' Did He? Well, one wouldn't guess it, not from the sight of our world here. The twilight was luminous, with a high, cold moon. I was wet, and caked with mud to the waist; but somehow, I don't know why, serene in heart. Perhaps it was because of the memory of the lad who was painting Christmas cards forty feet from the enemy."

TONIGHT I HAD coffee with Captain Jennat, down from the trenches for four days' repose. I am growing very fond of Jennat, the fat, pink, slant-eyed, serious, *gentil* little captain. 'Je crois que L'Amerique ne comprend pas notre guerre,' he said wistfully. And I have just finished writing my Christmas postcards from the Quart en Réserve. I was struck to laughter at the incongruity of the thing. The seventy-fives were roaring like wild bulls on the hills; rifles, mines, grenades, and what not filled in the interstices. *Christmas!* God save the day!"

ON THE SEVENTEENTH I was sent to La Fontaine de Père Ilarion, I have noted, in search of three wounded men — gassed. It is a beautiful name — the Spring of Ilarion. It was a spring in what should have been a sweetly wooded glen, damp-scented, and full of delicate imaginings of fairy creatures. But now it is a spring in what seems like a half-deserted mining camp in the heart of the Bois le Prêtre, with open trenches, like ugly, yellow wounds in the earth, ooze of mud, engines of destruction, masses of barbed wire. Over everything hung the horrible sense of impending disaster.

The ambulances come but seldom here; it is too near the firing line. The road stops short. As I hunted for the first-aid post, the bullets seemed to sing through the air much nearer than they really were. Ten yards away from the machine I saw a dummy put out to draw enemy fire. I moved the car with immoderate haste, I recall. But the journey, after all, was fruitless. The men were dead, the three of them. I was glad to leave the gloomy wood, to be out again in what seemed, oddly enough, safety.

By the roadside I marked a bush with very brilliant-orange winter berries. I have forgotten the name now. I shall come back to pick them on Christmas day, I declared, and then place them in the Glycine.

And farther on, so lonely and sad in the gray of the early twilight, I chanced upon soldiers carrying two long, narrow rough boxes — the bodies of a lieutenant and an adjutant killed the night before. How clearly that scene comes back to me today! They put them in my ambulance, and so they were carried in peace on to the little church in Monteauville, that shell-battered and broken home of God. I followed the bodies in, out of curiosity and respect. A French flag flung over the coffins suddenly and splendidly transformed them into a noble thing.

The tawdry place was dusky and cold. Flags hung on the altar amid the little flickering candles. The priest in crude, raucous tones began the mass before the gray-blue throng of the dead men's comrades; but the responses, accompanied by a wheezing organ in the loft, were chanted by a fine and manly voice that touched one's heart and somehow ennobled the dead. Afterward the coffins were carried out and put into a waiting cart. The night was gray, and the figures, bareheaded, were also gray, as seen through a fog. A soldier stepped out and spoke a fervent eulogy of the two dead men. His words were of no great significance, yet when he said "La France" he thrilled us. A splendid word, La France!

DECEMBER 20. "THE Boches began to shell Pont at ten o'clock this morning. The savage swish and zing and crash and bellow of the shrapnel and marmites never slackened until noon. As furious a bombardment as the town has ever received, one hears, and all this in the hope of killing a soldier or two or an old woman. This is precisely what happened. Plenty of damage was done, but the place is already so shot to bits that a little more or less matters nothing. A marmite plunged into the barber's shop and wrecked the back interior thoroughly. Half an hour after it was over I found a small boy ruefully shoveling into the tonsorial stove the coals shaken from it. 'Ces cochens!' he muttered. 'Eh bien, oui! Noël! Zut!'

"It is remarkable that one can shovel back coals after such roaring death in the air. As for me, I stood rather gingerly opposite the Glycine and talked with a lieutenant in a doorway. We popped in and out mechanically as the shells came over and broke. Odd thing to find yourself *being bombarded*. The officer said he was going on leave to spend Christmas with his wife and child at Paris. There were instants when he seemed unlikely to carry out his project, it seemed to me."

DECEMBER 22 has only a brief entry.

"The snow has turned to fine, icy rain. Jennat was killed today."

It is enough. I remember, how vividly, all of it. I was eating a half-cooked boiled potato and stew when they telephoned for an ambulance at Monteauville, the key to the trenches. I was 'next out.' I left that meal reluctantly; I was very hungry.

"It is for a corpse," said the *branquardier* at Poste 56, "to go to Blénod."

I asked idly who it was. A shoulder shrug.

"C'est un capitaine mort."

He pulled back the strip of muddy brown canvas over the stiff shape on the stretcher.

"Oh!" I stammered — "Oh, it is Jennat!" He was dead, struck an hour before ignobly in the back as he stood talking with his orderly at the door of his hut. His face was livid, and covered with scratches on which the blood had dried — a calm face, though a man's face. Dead, Jennat. We were friends. Something in him, something in me — you know how it is with friends.

134

And I was to take him to the train at Toul in my car, on the fifteenth of January. He was going home, on *permission*, to his wife and kiddies. Instead I took him to the church at Blénod. Dead, *permissionaire* forever, his last fight finished. Suddenly I knew what war is. Before that it had been a great adventure, something reckless and gallant and wild and splendid. I knew then; I know now. It is horrible, horrible.

I remembered the Christmas bush of brilliant-orange berries. I drove slowly onward till I found it. I got out then and cut a huge armful. They covered the whole stretcher glowingly. There was a lump in my throat all day, and there are tears close to my eyes as I write, though it was all long ago.

To die a death of one's own choosing, a decent one, is better than a foul wasting away with disease on a sickbed, I happened to say the last time I saw Jennat. "Ah, yes," he cried, "so much, much better!" I somehow think he felt that he was doomed. He gave me that sense. Poor Jennat!

DECEMBER 23. "RAW and rainy. Jennat's funeral was at nine o'clock at Blénod. The little, cold, ugly church was filled with officers and men of the 356th. They seemed very sorrowful over his death. *'Le bon capitaine,'* they said, and *'Charmant homme.'* A feeble old priest in black velvet whined the service; the soldiers shouldered the coffin, covered with the orange branches, the flag, his sword; and we followed, straggling through the mud to the cemetery. His colonel said of him at the open grave that he was a brave man, a gallant officer, a beloved friend. At the last all the officers in turn let fall some drops of holy water on the coffin in the shallow trench. *'Au revoir, Jennat,'* each man said very simply; and so presently it was all drearily over. It rained dismally, and in the distance there was heavy cannon-fire.

"Later on in the day Blénod was shelled."

DECEMBER 24. "R— and G— arrived this evening from Paris, having driven up new cars. They brought with them a Christmas dinner and gifts for us from friends of the section. It has been a horrible day of wind-blown rain. I have but just come back from a trip, up that long, winding road to the stormy plateau of Fey-en-Haye, to the first-aid post at Auberge St. Pierre. There was a dying man down in the cellar of the post. It was difficult to make any sort of speed to the surgery without lights in the heavy rain. The man was dead when we took him out of the ambulance, an ugly, yellow, bearded face; staring eyes; mouth open, showing knotty, brown teeth. His broken, bandaged arms were twisted over his head in a last writhe of agony. A strip of bandage had caught on his nose. Both legs were amputated, both arms broken; blood was clotted in his eyes. There was something oddly Egyptian, idol-like, in him as he lay in a fierce, hideous dignity of death and protest. Christmas eve!"

I scribbled that — how clear it comes back to me! — in the telephone room of the Glycine, that damp, dreary, dirty basement resort. I sat by the foul smelling oil-stove. It was very cold and raw that night. Q, the operator, and I occasionally talked bitterly of the war, of home, of Christmas.

I had in mind another Christmas eve I had spent in France in peace-time. It was at Marseilles. What a gay, ribald, reckless spirit ran through the place, up and down the tumultuous Cannobbière, that night! Peace, a seaport town, prosperity, home-come ships, and sailors; laughter and singing and wine and light-hearted women with smiling, love-lit eyes. And now this other. It was still France, but how terribly changed! Iron and fire and blood and steel, and a great beautiful winged soul.

As I fell asleep that night I remember thinking, a little ruefully, maybe, that this, after all, was the finer birthday for the young Lord Christ.

CHRISTMAS, AND AN icy, windy, devilish rain sweeping tempestuously over and under and through our war-wasted land. There was little enough in the sight or the sound or the sense of the day to create the holiday tradition; the grunt of cannon up there on the hill; soldiers, with pathetic makeshift protection against the pelting rain, straggling through the stretches of mud and ooze like Siberian exiles; the dull, disheartening business of war moving sluggishly on; creaking wagons; cursing drivers; patient ambulances lurching to and fro; *permissionaires* plodding station-ward, radiant of face, home in their eyes; *permissionaires* returning to their regiments, with faces glum and grim, home behind them. There was all the old,, unvarying, heartbreaking routine, with a touch of something that made it noble.

No one in the sector to which we were attached was wounded that day. That, maybe, was the real holiday note. At any rate, the ambulances and the drivers had no work. So when the two of us who were on duty that day at the railhead, Belleville, a godless hole, came back to the Glycine at five we found, in the dried-blood *salle*, a table that had a semblance of festivity and, despite the incongruity thereof, a note of Christmas, with green boughs and French flags, slim-necked bottles suggestive of white wine and sweet champagne, platters of amazing things — nothing less than cold turkey and ham, nuts, as I seem to remember, and little cakes. And, *bon Dieu de France!* khaki-clad drivers, surprisingly washed and shaved and brushed to unrecognizable clarity! On the edge of it were Mme. Marin and little Jeanne giggling and chattering and complimenting in the gayest and friendliest mood imaginable.

I must tell you that Marin mère with her *petite fillette* had lived in the villa before the war as housekeeper. When the first in-rush of the Germans drove her employers away, along with the rest of, the city, she stayed calmly on. "Pourquoi faut-il m'en aller?" she asked tartly. Of all the groups of military who occupied the house in turn she loved best *les Américains*. She cooked for us, dosed us when we were ill, joked with us, scolded, and wept. Dear old Mere Marin, fat, friendly, bourgeoise, sweet, and brave! Pretty little thirteen-year-old, modest, deft Jeanne, so apt at picking up our English! I wonder where they are today. And is some one making *bonne fête* for them tonight in the battered old Glycine? I hope so; but I fear there is little Christmas now for them.

And Mère Marin had an ear for shells. What an ear! By the sound of them in the air she knew infallibly if they came or went, their size, and their probable nearness. She took them as calmly as if they were bumblebees.

But to get back to our Christmas.

At each place there was a tiny colored card that said beautifully (alas! untruthfully) *L'Année de la Victoire!* And each man of us had been given, marked with his name, a little officer's trunk in which one discovered samples of shaving-soap and toothpaste, brass collar-buttons, a cravat, and a tidy Christmas card. All, it turned out, came from an enchanting lady from Philadelphia, whose name I have forgotten, but whose spirit and whose heaven-inspired gifts I shall never cease to keep green in memory. Oh, she went still further, it developed later; for she had added to all the rest a gramophone, which was produced at a fitting moment and which played incessantly and with almost a divine fire, so we felt, from then on. I dare say it is still at it. The "Roosevelt March" and the "Marche Lorraine" were its *chefs d'oeuvres* beyond any question.

Well, it was a gay meal, recklessly, happily so, and though it may seem incredible, it ended with a huge plum pudding.

It ended, too, with something very grave and, as I think of it now, very beautiful. The festival meal and the gifts were forgotten in the face of it. For it was, oh, not strangely, of those events which lift men, if ever so briefly, out of their daily selves into unseen things. Our chief of section was called to the telephone. He came back — we all saw it — with saddened face.

"Fellows," he said slowly, "Richard Hall of Section III has been killed, blown off his car by a stray shell in the Vosges. He is the first of us all to go."

We stood very silently and soberly about the table. Such news drove home abruptly, cruelly — the more abruptly and more cruelly by reason of our Christmas-day gaieties — just what being there involved to us, to those who loved us. Very often we had jested and joked about death. None of us was a coward, I think; but — Hall — dead — the first of the lot of us — dead — so far from home — Christmas.

And then some one, raising his glass, said quietly:

"Boys, let's drink to him, the first of us to lay down his life for France. Here's to Dick Hall, good old scout!"

So we drank, and I think no man there that night, where danger and death were always brooding darkly, but failed to feel the dignity and honor of his calling.

A long time after, the mother of Richard Hall said to a friend of mine — said with clear, sad, gentle eyes, "I am glad to give my boy to so great a cause." And we, on the edge of the sinister Bois le Prêtre, when the news of her boy's death came to us that Christmas day, felt, too, somehow, somewhere within us, that the cause was great, was ours.

So Christmas, after all, ended solemnly. We sat about in knots and talked in low voices of intimate and far-away things. We were very closely drawn together, more closely than brothers. Home and our own people were very distant, unreachably distant. So it ended.

LATE THAT NIGHT I stood alone for a time under the starry sky of that strange hell we inhabited. Oddly enough, I felt, so I recall, a calmness and a courage, even a sort of happiness, new and strange. Though its approaches might be loud and frightening, I knew again that "the ways of death are silent and serene." An honorable death, a death of one's own choosing, for an ideal, for a cause.

And — how vivid the memory of it! I turned away with this on my lips:

> "From too much love of living.
> From hope and fear set free.
> We thank with brief thanksgiving
> Whatever gods may be.
> That no life lives forever.
> That dead men rise up never.
>
> And even the weariest river
> Winds somewhere safe to sea."

139

A Christmas City in the Old South.

BY WINIFRED KIRKLAND

From 'The North American Review,' December 1923

THE ONLY way to visit old Salem of the old South is with a child's heart for luggage. Otherwise this old town in the middle of North Carolina may lie before your eyes actual enough, with its old streets, its old houses, its old Square, its old Home Church as its inmost core, and Salem may welcome you with the gentle, unobtrusive courtesy peculiarly its own; but unless you have learned the wisdom that knows how to put away grown-up things, you cannot really enter the Christmas city.

In Salem, of all places I have ever seen, it is easiest to drop from one's shoulders the crippling pack of maturity and become once again a little child stepping along a Christmas road. Of all places it is easiest in Salem to forget the jangle of faiths and of no-faiths that have deadened our ears, to slip away from the clangor of an age proud and fevered as ancient Rome, and to listen to the confidence of old carols ringing along moonlit dreamy streets, mysterious with the black of magnolia and of boxwood, or to hear floating down from the church belfry high up under the stars the silver melody of the ancient horns which, better than any other instrument, express the soul of the Moravian church. A most musical religion it must seem to every visitor who yields his spirit to the spirit of Moravian Salem. Not only the church liturgy but also the everyday life of the community is keyed to old tunes that date back, some of them, to the Bohemia of five centuries ago, and were familiar in Moravian households in the days when John Huss was martyred for the beauty of his faith.

There is a spell on southern Salem, the spell not of a dead past but of a living one, constantly revitalized, so that, as one walks these uneven red brick pavements, one is haunted by memories of long past Christmases, thoughts of those far times when in secrecy and fear the Hidden Seed kept its feast of candles and of anthems, thoughts of happier festivals in Saxony where young Count Zinzendorf offered the heretics the refuge city of Herrnhut, thoughts of brave long ago love feasts right here, when a tiny, intrepid band of colonists sang its Christmas chorales in the midst of endless miles of wilderness, while wolves nosed and howled at the cabin door. Along with these Moravian memories come thronging recollections of one's own child-hood Christmases in all their unforgotten wizardry, so that here in Christmas Salem I seem to be walking again the midnight aisle which leads through a great wood of fir trees looming black against high stars. Just as at five years old, I am aware again of mystery and danger and bewilderment lurking far off in the forest; but along the Christmas roadway there is no fear, only joy and magic, for it lies straight as a shaft of silver through the black wood, and along it troops of youngsters go dancing onward. At the instant that the children pass, each dark, bordering fir tree becomes bright with tinsel and candles, and along the spicy twigs gay little bells stir and tinkle. From time to time there come snatches of happy chants echoed among the tall dim trunks. Since the wayfarers are children, they know that the soft, unearthly radiance upon the road before them is the long beam from a star not yet seen because it hangs so low above a stable cave, and they know, too, that their silver path is leading all child feet toward that star. Small difference for children between that spirit light of Bethlehem and the merry twinkle of Christmas tree candles.

For them, readily enough, their own carol singing mingles with the voices of herald angels, and even Santa Claus himself, all ruddy and kind, may steal to the stable door and gaze in on a Divine Baby. Even so are Christmas faith and Christmas fancy interwoven in old Salem, where white headed men and women still have their Christmas trees, and still with their own hands construct beneath the green boughs the wonderful Christmas "putzes"; for while we who are visitors must retread in stumbling unfamiliarity the Christmas path, the Moravians of old Salem have always kept straight and clear within their hearts the child road toward the star.

When, a few days before Christmas, I arrived in Salem, people told me I had missed what for Moravians is always the opening key to the Yuletide season. For unnumbered years there has always been sung on the Sunday before Christmas the anthem of *The Morning Star*, written in the later seventeenth century, and set to music in the nineteenth. Although I never heard choir and congregation unite in its mighty joy, I seemed, during my two weeks' visit, always to be catching its echoes, as if the strains of Christmas minstrels had come floating back to me where, unseen in the distance, they had passed on before, along the silver lit highway, so that the words and the music of *The Morning Star* voice for me the innermost spirit of a Moravian Christmas.

The anthem has both the quaintness of old Germany and the vigorous confidence of the new world, so that the old words and the new are equally expressive of the unchanging faith of present-day Salem, while the music vibrates with the sheer child-gladness of its praise:

> *Morgenstern auf Finster Nacht*
> *Der die Welt voll Freude macht,*
> *Jesulein, 0 kommherein,*
> *Leucht in meines Hertzens Schrein.*

When, in stanza two, music and words swell out into grandeur, it is as if, out of the black forest mystery of life, some hidden joyous congregation suddenly pealed forth a psalm to the mounting Christmas dawn:

A CHRISTMAS CITY IN THE OLD SOUTH

Morning star, thy glory bright
Far exceeds the sun's clear light;
Jesus be, constantly,
More than thousand suns to me.

For the holiday guest there slowly emerges upon that glamorous woodland roadway of his child memories a silver lighted city, gradually shaping into the everyday reality of actual Salem. As I look out from the window of the little gray cottage that harbors me, there become sharply etched against the mistiness of dreams the tall water oaks of the old red brick Square, the domes of boxwood against old walls of buff stucco or of brick, the stretching flat white rows of gravestones holly trimmed, the white belfry of the Home Church, where in Christmas week I heard little boys, high up there in the soft December sunshine, sound the trombone announcement of death. So unobtrusive and yet so sweet were those strains out of the sky, so blent with the Christmas air, that I listened to them for some time supposing them merely carol-singing floating out from some home where the family had regathered for Christmas.

On one side the little cottage looks forth on the sunny graveyard where Moravians keep their dead too close to life for any sadness, and on the other side it nestles to the prouder, taller buildings of the Square, laid out in the seventeen-sixties by founders who established Salem as the central city of their Wachovian grant of seventy thousand acres, to be built and to be kept a city meet for their faith. The solid eighteenth century houses still remain, skillfully adapted to modern usage, or unobtrusively altered. Half of Salem traces its ancestry back to those earlier days, and all of Salem keeps alive, both in family life and in public, the traditions and the customs of its unforgotten builders.

Perhaps it is only in our own South that so gentle and half romantic a faith could have found so gracious a flowering as is typified in the Easter and the Christmas customs of this Salem of North Carolina. There is a blending of native warmth and glow and kindliness in the

144

spirit of this Southern Province of the Moravian Church. The first colonists came seeking a mild climate and friendly neighbors, and found both. For a hundred and fifty years Salem has been true to its first purpose. Long ago it was a little refuge city of peace in the wilderness, and still today it offers its benediction for all who seek to penetrate beyond the mere externals of a locality into the inner sanctities of tradition. Long ago a brave little band kept to their secure daily round of work and worship, amid perils of Indian attack and the backwash of Continental armies, and freely gave their hospitality to everyone that asked it; and today the mind of those first settlers still dominates and moulds the life of the city. Yesterday and now the people of Salem have possessed both the art of shrewd adjustment to the contemporary and the power to withdraw from all its fever and conflict into the peace of a child faith. With quaint literalness those early founders looked upon themselves as all members of one family, and today one of the strongest impressions of any visitor is that of a great household, close bound in sympathy, and all turning toward the old Home Church as to a central hearthside, while up and down the worn old streets there moves the form of one still young at eighty, who in himself is host and shepherd and father of all the city.

One wonders if the inhabitants of Salem fully realize their high privilege of living in a community which both expresses their religion and preserves the finest traditions of their ancestors. In these bewildering days it is the lot of most idealists to live in a solitude, unable, amid the surrounding mists, to distinguish the shapes of their fellow believers. But in Salem people have the sacred advantage of dwelling with those who constantly share and reinforce each other's faith as naturally as they have shared each other's childhood and each other's memories of the old Infant School. Probably Moravians do not dream with what strange nostalgia a visitor listens to persons who treat God conversationally, who talk of Him as spontaneously as a little boy speaks of that splendid comrade he calls Daddy. Normally enough, naturally enough, has the Moravian spirit been able to strike deep roots in our own South, for there religion is still a custom unquestioned, and leisure can still be found for an obsolete, Old World culture, and intellect still bows in reverence before the soul. In old Salem of the old South there can be no blur upon the radiant confidence of the Christmas story, no smirch upon the silver purity of that far lit path toward Bethlehem's cave.

In Salem I feel myself to be sometimes in Cranford, sometimes in Barchester, while all reminiscence of those two familiar hometowns of the fancy is touched by an atmosphere sacred to Salem. From one window of my room I can gaze up the long, silent avenue, forbidden to all vehicles, that skirts the high ivy hung picket fence of the graveyard. Even in December the graveyard grass is vivid in the sunshine. I am so near that I can almost see the crimson berries of the holly wreaths laid on the little flat marble slabs. Cedar Avenue lies, a white path at the heart of Salem. On one side of it are gateways whose sunny arches, blazoned with texts of hope, stand bright against the mystery of shadowy spruce and cedar massed beyond the triumphant little gravestones, marching forever onward in steadfast Christmas faith. Along Cedar Avenue I have watched a funeral pro-cession move with confident tread, while the trombone strains floated forth delicate and clear upon the New Year's morning.

Another window of my room looks toward the old Square, toward the Bishop's home beside the Bishop's church, toward the aging buildings that still bear names witnessing to the deep Moravian reverence for the family as a holy entity — the Sisters' House, the House of the Single Brethren, the Widows' House.

A simple vital reverence for tradition is as characteristic of each individual home as it is of the larger home life of the church congregation. In the tiny cottage that offers me hospitality there is a little wooden rocking chair carefully treasured. One turns it up to find on the bottom in a handwriting too alive ever to be forgotten these words, "This rocker was used by mother to rock all her nine babies to sleep from 1828-1844. Keep it in the family." There lies on this little chair a touch of that personal immortality that the home-going dead must value; and yet it is only a little wooden rocker, tawny drab, and finely lined like an old parchment, or an old face. It has no arms, therefore had no bumps for little heads. It has spreading legs and rockers, and on each rocker is painted a bunch of fading wild roses. All the little home is gentle with old memories. Each morning at the close of breakfast I listen first to the daily reading from the Moravian Textbook for the year, the custom of the Textbook dating back to Count Zinzendorf; and after the Textbook comes the reading from birthday and memory books. As I listen, a kindly past made up of small family events becomes vital for me, the guest. Yet the little cottage is alive to the present as well as to the past. The neighbor children blow in and out, all ruddy with ball playing. The Moravian is a children's church, its services crowded with jolly youngsters, seated as happily beside their parents as seedlings grow around a tree. To Moravian children the story of a children's Friend is no dead tale. The rosy seven-year old Harold who comes flying so often to our door has a hearty affection for Santa Claus, but with that Other he is even more familiar. A few weeks before this last Christmas a little playmate died. Harold was puzzled by the sorrow of the grown-ups and protested, "But Louise has gone to Jesus, and she will be there for His birthday."

The star faith of Salem is today no dying creed, but an imperishable growth in the hearts of young men. One has constantly the sense of a past neither decayed nor decadent, being entrusted to younger hands that are vigorous and willing. One seems to witness the very act of a sacramental transmission, the faith of one great united family being handed down to its sons. In the big house next to our cottage I saw on Christmas Eve the table spread for a family party of thirty-two. There was the cushioned seat for the grandmother at the head, and the high chairs for the smallest grandchildren. Down through the center amid the heaped holly and carnations extended a long green board holding eighty blazing candles, the long frame having been originally made for the Bishop's birthday, and now borrowed in Salem's characteristic neighborly fashion. But it is not the old time Yuletide glow of the stretching Christmas table that will longest remain in my memory, but the chanted grace I heard later from my window, a grace composed by the English John Cennick nearly two hundred years ago:

Be present at our table, Lord;
Be here and everywhere adored,
From Thy all-bounteous hand our food
May we receive with gratitude.

We humbly thank Thee, Lord, our God,
For all thy gifts on us bestowed;
And pray Thee graciously to grant,
The food which day by day we want.

More impressive than the rich harmony of men's voices ringing out upon the starlit evening was their utter reverence; and these, it must be emphasized, are the voices of young men, young bankers, young merchants and lawyers of that Twin City which is made up of two united towns, one new, one old, named on the maps Winston-Salem. These are the torchbearers whose first memory of their faith is as toddlers brought to the Children's Christmas Eve Love Feast. There are the young fathers who now bring their own toddlers to hear the Bishop tell once again to children, as for forty-five years he has been telling it, the child story of a star.

There are persons who walk the Christmas lighted path through earth's black mystery not on one day of the year only, but on all the days of all the years. The Magi were subtle students, keen men and free minded, rich with the long inherited treasures of the intellect. It was their science, not their superstition, that revealed to them the birth of a new light in the heavens. Bishop Rondthaler's eyes are a seer's eyes, clear blue lanterns at eighty. His face is of the type transmitted only through long generations of the finely educated. There is not a child in Salem who does not know Bishop Rondthaler's smile.

Bishop Rondthaler's voice. How many times he must have sung that old glad anthem, which each year on its appointed Sunday rings out upon the Christmas road of Salem:

Morning Star, my soul's true light,
Tarry not, dispel my night;
Jesus mine, in me shine.
Fill my heart with light divine.

The Children's Love Feast of Christmas Eve is a custom as old as Salem, and older. More than a hundred and fifty years ago, when Wachovia was still a forest wilderness dark with perils of wolves and bears and hostile Indians, the Moravian Brethren of the little settlements of Bethabara and Bethania welcomed to the children's love feasts not only their own children, but those of their neighbors. The old records come down to us all bright and warm with Christmas hospitality. In the diary of the Bethabara congregation of December, 1760, one reads:

"On the 5th [of December, 1760] it was reported that the Indians were killing again on the Catawba. Br. Ettwein had a talk with a Tuscarora. On Christmas Day the English children from the mill came to see our Christmas decoration, they were so poorly clad that it would have moved a stone to pity. We told them why we rejoiced like children and gave to each a piece of cake. In Bethania Br. Ettwein held a Love Feast for the 24 children there, at the close of the service each received a pretty Christmas verse and a ginger cake, the first they had ever seen."

In 1761, one first reads of the giving of lighted tapers, that custom never yet broken. In the account written December 24, 1770, one can still hear those far off carols, still see the twinkle of candles held high by youngsters dancing homeward along the dark wood-paths: "At 6 P.M. a Love Feast was held for the children, appropriate hymns were sung, and small lighted candles were distributed, which they joyfully carried home, still burning."

A CHRISTMAS CITY IN THE OLD SOUTH

As those first settler children must have come all eager to those long ago celebrations of their Moravian neighbors, so today the Christmas Eve crowd is composed as much of non-Moravians as of church members, all flocking to the old Home Church of their city. For half an hour before the doors could be opened, while the sunshine of the late afternoon poured over us, I waited with a happy throng, fathers and mothers and grandparents, and youngsters of every age from one year to twelve. As soon as the doors admitted us, the wide arc of each pew was instantly filled, but the little low heads were not all visible except as they popped up to peer around, little brown or blond heads, bobbed or meticulously curled. The church hummed with little voices. Now and then a baby protested sharply against being repressed by some solicitous mother, but for the most part all the noise was happy. The long window which showed children crowding to Jesus' welcome was still clear in the afternoon light, which as the service proceeded dimmed to shadowy evening. All the Christmas decoration focused the eye upon the picture above the choir platform which extends across the front of the church. In a deep green frame of shining laurel and spruce there shines out each year the same ruddy illumination of Correggio's Nativity. On each Christmas Eve every child in the congregation looks up to see, all bathed in glowing light, a mother bending over the Christ Baby in his stable.

As if it had been quaint home incense, the aroma of the love feast coffee is fragrant through the church. There is rustling, there is chatter of children, and yet also there is the restraint of a great reverence. Then a hush, and everyone is listening. Somewhere high and far away there is music, silvery announcement from the sky. Grown-up hands touch the little ones to quiet, that all may hear. It is the trombone players in the belfry, but how easily it might have been the herald angels! Soft at first, then in growing volume, the organ takes up and continues those strains from overhead. The service moves on all musically, old carols, jubilant anthems, but because it is a children's service in a children's church it is brief and simple. It is not long before the two doors at the right beneath the gallery swing open, and a reverent procession of women all in white enters, bearing the baskets of love feast buns. There follows a line of men carrying great wooden trays of the straight white mugs of love feast coffee. Quietly as in some happy sacrament, each child is given his bun and mug. Seated in front, close to them, sharing their love feast meal, the Bishop looks forth on his children. Gently his voice breaks upon the rustling, and the subdued chatter of little lips: "Fathers and mothers who at this moment are guiding a child's hand, as he eats his love feast, one too young to know what he is doing, pray each one of you that at this instant Jesus Himself may come and be near your little child with His Christmas blessing."

When the bun is eaten, the coffee drunk, and the mugs collected and taken away by the silent procession, the Bishop rises. The church is growing dark with the stealing shadows of twilight. Never has the Bishop's telling of the old story been twice the same. To him it is forever new. He speaks on the brief text, "Yet for our sakes He became poor." The babbling of little tongues grows still. Young eyes grow wide, looking into the Bishop's. In words instinctively pictorial he tells us there was once in Heaven a marvelous house, golden and splendid, where Jesus lived with His Father, surrounded by love and tenderness and beauty beyond any telling. Outside of this house were stately trees, and lovely flowers, and darting birds of rainbow colors. All about Jesus in His house were angels more than you could count, and these angels asked only one thing, to serve Him. To wait on Jesus was the sole wish of all these regiments of angels in this beautiful house in Heaven. Yet all this love and all this royal splendor Jesus left, that He might come a little baby, too poor to have a cradle, a baby born in a stable, laid to sleep among the cattle. He came to us, all poor, to see whether we would love Him for Himself alone, without any riches of money or of power. And still today, as He lies there, a little baby in a stable, He is asking, "Children, will you love me for myself alone?" And if we do love Him for Himself alone, pleads the Bishop's voice, remembering how He loved us enough to leave His splendid home to come to us, if we love Him and try, each child of us here in this church today, to please Him, then some day He will take us home, to live with Him in His beautiful house in Heaven, forever.

Gently the twilight wraps us in darkness, more carols ring through the old church, then on each side of the organ in front of us, a door opens and two women in white appear, the van of a procession which moves down the platform steps and through the aisles. Each woman carries a lighted candle, and each pair is followed by a man bearing a great tray of blazing tapers. The women distribute the candles, one to every child in the congregation. The giving of the candles closes the service. Theirs is the only light in the darkness as we rise for the Bishop's blessing, and then afterward pour out beneath the old hooded doorway into the starlit Christmas Eve. Looking back one sees still faintly discernible the figures in that high window which against the outdoor darkness and mystery reveals Jesus blessing little children.

The Moravian is a children's church by no accident, but by long conviction, as the Bishop himself once explained to me. When, in the early eighteenth century, the ancient Unitas Fratrum of Bohemia experienced its great revival at Herrnhut under the protection of young Count Zinzendorf, there suddenly occurred — as it appears, quite spontaneously — a great wave of religious enthusiasm among the children. The quaint touching account comes down to us in the words of ten-year-old diarists. Ever since that time, says the Bishop, "Our reverence for childhood has been founded on the belief that a child can be as good a Christian as a grown-up — and perhaps a little better." In Salem the children's Christmas Eve Love Feast, and the Children's Memorabilia Service at New Year's, are made fully as important as the corresponding celebrations for adults. Just as, in the afternoon, the children come to receive their Christmas candles, so, a few hours later, the grown-ups gather in their turn, for their reverent Christmas love feast.

Except for its deeper solemnity, the evening love feast is a repetition of that of the afternoon. The crowded church is a body of men and women assembled once more to gaze with the Bishop at that shining picture of the Nativity. Again there floats down upon the hushed congregation the faint, silver music from the belfry, sacred minstrelsy sounding out of the darkness to be taken up by the confident organ. As the congregation rises, the whole building resounds with the joy of the anthem, and when this dies away, the Bishop's quiet voice asks us to continue standing while he reads Luke's account of that long ago night in Bethlehem. There in the old Home Church of old Salem, the story of the first Christmas becomes instinct with a mystical reality. Later in the service, which, like all the ritual of the Moravian church, consists far more of praise than of prayer, the Bishop speaks to us of that undying narrative, and as his steadfast belief leads us, children following his eighty-year-old guidance, back to that holy birthplace of his faith, it is as if we trod once again a silver pathway bright against all gloom, all doubt, while sturdy shepherds and glistening angels come thrusting aside the darkness to companion us along the road to Bethlehem.

The Bishop reminds us that a great literary critic once pronounced Luke's Gospel the most beautiful book in the world. Of this book the second chapter is the most beautiful of all. Thoughtful readers of it must remember always that Luke was a Greek doctor, highly educated, scientific in dealing with his sources. He was Paul's physician, and Paul was after his conversion the familiar friend of the apostles in Jerusalem, undoubtedly the friend of John at whose home Mary lived. We may well believe, therefore, that the story of Christ's birth, as we have it in Luke's Gospel, is His mother's story, coming down to us how near, how quick and alive! Between us and Mary's own voice telling it only two people, Paul who transmitted the account, Luke who wrote it down! The Bishop points out how tender and how holy is the chronicle with details only Jesus' mother could have known. As the most sacred thing in our physical life is the relation of a human mother to her human child, so it is most fitting that the story of the birth of a divine Child should be a record from a mother's lips of mother love.

A CHRISTMAS CITY IN THE OLD SOUTH

Beneath the illumined scene of that Nativity which focuses for-ever all Christmas worship on the holiness of a family group, we eat the Christmas love feast that symbolizes by our sharing of food and drink together our close-knit membership in one great family. In utter quiet, in utter reverence, the procession of white clad girls and women moves slowly down the aisles distributing to every one pres-ent the love feast buns. According to custom, each one of us wraps our bun in a tiny napkin brought for the purpose. On one corner of the napkin is embroidered a cross. Then at the entrance of the men with the great laden trays, the high white mugs of coffee are passed from hand to hand along the wide-curving pews. The solemn hush is gently broken by the Bishop's words pointing out our unconscious courtesy, courtesy which is like Christ's own, he believes, and which cements for this holy hour the intimacy of our kinship. He asks us, while we wait, to sing, "Blest be the tie that binds — " According to old custom the Bishop has been the first served, seated by the com-munion table, close to his people, as always, and wearing, as always, merely the ordinary dress of his fellow worshippers. When every one has been served, then the Bishop and congregation together eat the love feast bun, drink the love feast coffee, while the organ peals forth its Christmas joy.

Musically the service passes on to the candle giving. All the church is darkened. As in the afternoon, to right and left of the organ in front of us, doors open, and two by two the white-dressed women, holding each her burning candle, and the men carrying the long trays that blaze with light, enter and pass down all aisles and through the curving gallery. Beginning with the Bishop, they give to everyone in the church a lighted taper, slim, green, girdled with its frill of crim-son paper. Briefly the Bishop explains the meaning of the Moravian Christmas candles. "As Jesus came that He might be a shining light for us in a black world, so let each of us bear a light for Him."

When everyone has received a candle the procession moves back up the converging aisles, remounts the steps of the platform, but does not pass out. All the middle space in front of the organ is a screen of spruce and holly and dark glistening laurel, from the centre of which the Nativity scene glows just above the Bishop's head, as he stands facing us, his figure discernible only by the light of the taper in his hand. In front of the choir doors, to right and left, are grouped the women all in white except for a sprig of holly on the breast. Behind them stand the men on whose trays is still left a mass of blazing candles rosy-trimmed. In the gallery and in the body of the church, people have become invisible in the dark, but the curve of every pew above and below is outlined by a shining row of tapers against the blackness. All in silence we have risen. The Bishop speaks, "Let each of us at this instant lift high his candle, so that Jesus from heaven may look down and see the shining of our light for Him." Then as we stand, each holding high his tiny gleaming taper, the Bishop's voice, melodious from out the engulfing shadows, leads us all as we sing, "Praise God, from Whom all blessings flow,"

As we leave the church, the moonlight is pouring down on the old roofs, the old streets. Cedar Avenue lies like a shaft of silver beyond the church door. Shadows of bare trees are etched black on the worn pavements. Moonlight glistens on the ivy walls, on the long leaves of the magnolia trees, on the towering domes of boxwood. Little streets and old alleys opening on the Square are black tunnels of mystery. The tracery of the water oaks is delicately clear against a sky flooded with silver. Salem lies as still beneath the Christmas moon as if it were a city in some old world legend. In the hush there goes still ringing sweet within one's mind the music of ancient trumpets from the sky, the melody of a clear voice, reading a mystical story. Today's rushing progress seems as far away as the clangor of the trolley on the next street. If on one long ago December night some Roman traveler, posting from city to city on a tour through ancient Palestine, had stopped, puzzled, to investigate a strange light coming from a stable cave on the outskirts of a little hill town, and if, as he approached that light, the sky above his head had suddenly been riven by angels singing of

155

a new born god, how afterward when he went back to that bustling, imperial centre of the world would he have related that portentous incident of his journeyings? In what words comprehensible to that proud, fevered Rome of Augustus Caesar could a Roman traveler have translated his impressions of a far away little village, made holy by faith, a far away little village lying in peace beneath a silver flooded Christmas sky? Would such a traveler, as the crowded, noisy years went on, cease trying to explain to anyone that strange vision, even while in his heart the picture of that midnight village grew always more vivid, more arresting?

To one traveler turned aside last Christmas time from the clamorous streets of today, to walk for a little while the Christmas road through old Salem, the memory of the Christmas city grows ever more significant, more challenging. The glory of imperial Rome has faded into darkness, but does the road to Bethlehem still lie silver clear, beckoning to wise men? As long as little children shall be born, shall there be reborn each Christmas the faith in a God who became a baby? Ringing through midnight streets, echoed among the black overshadowing branches of mystery, shall there sound forever, as always at Christmas time in old Salem, the praise of a great light?

> Thy glad beams, Thou morning Star,
> Cheer the nations near and far;
> Thee we own. Lord alone,
> Man's great Savior, God's dear Son.

An American Christmas in Many Tongues.

BY JULIA SEARING LEAYCRAFT

From 'The Outlook,' December 1923

Has the reader ever stopped to think, when he sat down to his good old-fashioned Christmas dinner — turkey, cranberry sauce, pie, and all — that in thousands of homes, American homes, all over this country the American Christmas has a very different aspect? And on Christmas Eve when the tree is alight, and on Christmas morning when the presents are distributed, what do you think is going on in the families of the thousands of adopted Americans all over the country?

In the International Institutes, the clubs of the Y.W.C.A., to which girls from all the nations of Europe belong, the great desire has always been to preserve the best of the old country and at the same time teach the best that American can offer. For many years these clubs have given international Christmas parties, with Christmas customs of the various countries called to mind by costume and folk plays. Girls of all nationalities join together in tableaux and plays representing the old story dear to the people of every land. And in the course of the evening a particular custom of each nation is lovingly represented by its daughters in this new land of their adoption.

What could be more beautiful than the Polish custom of not

FOLK DANCES AT AN "INTERNATIONAL PARTY" — SEVEN NATIONALITIES REPRESENTED IN COSTUME. ONE OF THESE DANCERS IS A BOHEMIAN OR CZECH, THE OTHER IS A SLOVAK. DIRECTLY BEHIND THEM IS A RUSSIAN IN BRIDAL COSTUME, AND BEHIND HER A POLISH GIRL. ON THE LEFT ARE ITALIANS, A BULGARIAN, AND A HUNGARIAN. THEY WERE ALL STUDENTS IN THE Y.W.C.A., ARE ALL WELL EDUCATED, AND MANY ARE TALENTED MUSICIANS AND ARTISTS.

sitting down to dinner on Christmas Eve until the evening star is in the sky? And those who partake of the bountiful Polish Christmas dinner see hanging from under the fine white cloth of the table bits of straw reminiscent of the first Christmas, while a vacant chair is left at every Polish table for the little baby born that day so many hundred years before.

As any American-Bohemian would tell you, preparations for Christmas are far-reaching in Czechoslovakia. The children, with the assistance of the very old people, plan and built what is known as a "Bethlehem" — a realistic presentation of the Nativity. Sometimes it is arranged on a tiny stage. These Bethlehems are often handed down from generation to generation, and great care is expended in carving, painting, and dressing the figures and keeping them in repair. Groups of children go from house to house singing ancient carols full of poetic beauty and musical grace, and are rewarded with red-cheeked apples, handfuls of nuts, big slices of Christmas cake. The leaders of the singers, who are usually dressed to represent the Three Kings from the East, mark with three crosses each house that has been visited.

Our sisters and brothers of Italy do all they can to preserve the customs of the sunny land in celebrating Christmas, though it is impossible in the crowded cities here to continue many of the things they used to do. But the religious significance of the day is never lost sight of. At twelve o'clock on Christmas Eve the churches are filled, and the people often go from church to church to see and to worship before the *Presepio*, a carving in wood or stone of the holy family. In the villages of southern Italy there are shrines on the outside of the houses containing *Presepios*, and a professional bagpiper dressed in gay holiday colors goes from shrine to shrine playing his Christmas tunes, followed by a host of children and any who during the past year have received a special favor from God.

To a Great, Christmas is a holy day. There is no giving of gifts on the Christ Child's birthday; that is reserved for New Year's, and then only among the most intimate friends of the family. But for Christmas, which comes, according to the Greek calendar, thirteen days later than ours, the Greeks have carefully preserved the old customs which grew on the sunny slopes of Greek orchard hills. Every house is cleaned and white-washed. Every member of the family has new clothes, and supplies of fruits of all kinds that in the old country were gathered from the orchards and gardens and hung in the cellars are never touched till Christmas morning.

In Norway, Sweden, and Denmark the people begin to celebrate at six o'clock on December 24, and continue until January 7. During that time no one may enter a home without eating and drinking, or bad luck with attend that house during the year. Christmas Eve is the gala

"THE IMMIGRANT MADONNA" — AN INTERNATIONAL GROUP: BABY, AMERICAN,; MOTHER, ITALIAN; ANGELS, GREEK AND POLISH. FROM A TABLEAU GIVEN AT AN INTERNATIONAL INSTITITUTE FOR YOUNG WOMEN, ONE OF THE CLUBS OF THE Y.W.C.A.

night; then the feast is spread, and every family, no matter how poor, must have its *risengröd*, its goose, and its *aebleskiver* (dessert). In the *risengröd*, which is made of rice, almonds are hidden, and the lucky child who finds one receives a prize and the certainty of good luck. After the feast comes the tree, a big one, and always in the center of the room, with its gay colors, candles, and gifts. It is too beautiful to take calmly! Everyone joins hands and dances about the tree, singing and laughing. The gifts are distributed, when possible, by *Julenisse* himself (known to us as Santa Claus).

Christmas Eve is the great time of celebrations for Russians. The Christmas tree is hidden. The doors are opened and the children burst into the room, the tree all alight. When the candles are burned down, the children blow them out. Pouf! Then with wild uproar the tree is

160

torn to pieces, and the trinkets and presents are divided among the children. The feast follows with cold meats and cakes, all rich with nuts and raisins. And on Christmas Day no Russian table is complete without a nice fat little roast pig.

Our Armenian-Americans have adopted our American Christmas in their families, but in their churches they continue the old religious customs. They, too, follow the Greek calendar, and in Armenia on Christmas morning, long before daylight, the streets are filled with people on their way to church, each carrying his own lantern.

It is not only in the International Institutes, but in all the foreign communities of our great American cities, that these different customs are being remembered and observed to do honor to the birthday of the greatest Friend of the poor and oppressed.

Christmas and the Literature of Disillusion.

BY SAMUEL MCCORD CROTHERS

From 'The Atlantic Monthly,' December 1906

What makes the book so cross?" asked the youngest listener, who had for a few minutes, for lack of anything better to do, been paying some slight attention to the reading that was intended for her elders.

It was a question which we had not been bright enough to ask. We had been plodding on with the vague idea that it was a delightful book. Certainly the subject was agreeable. The writer was taking us on a ramble through the less frequented parts of Italy. He had a fine descriptive power and made us see the quiet hill towns, the old walls, the simple peasants, the white Umbrian cattle in the fields. It was just the sort of thing that should have brought peace to the soul; but it didn't.

The author had the trick of rubbing his subject the wrong way. Everything he saw seemed to suggest something just the opposite. When every prospect pleased, he took offense at something that wasn't there. He was himself a favored man of leisure; and could go where he pleased and stay as long as he liked. Instead of being content with a short Pharisaic prayer of thanksgiving that he was not as other men, he turned to berate the other men, who in New

York were, at that very moment, rushing up and down the crowded streets in the frantic haste to be rich. He treated their fault as his misfortune. Indeed, it was unfortunate that the thought of their haste should spoil the serenity of his contemplation. His fine sense for the precious in art led him to seek the untrodden ways. He indulged in bitter gibes at the poor taste of the crowd. In some faraway church, just as he was getting ready to enjoy a beautifully faded picture on the wall, he caught sight of a tourist. He was only a mild-mannered man with an apologetic air, as one who would say, "Let me look too. I mean no harm."

It was a meek effort at appreciation, but to the gentleman who wrote the book it was an offense. Here was a spy from "the crowd," an emissary of "the modern." By and by the whole pack would be in full cry and the lovely solitude would be no more. Then the author wandered off through the olives, where under the unclouded Italian sky he could see the long line of the Appenines, and there he meditated on the insufferable smoke of Sheffield and Pittsburg.

The young critic was right, the author was undoubtedly "cross." In early childhood this sort of thing is well understood, and called by its right name. When a small person starts the day in a contradictory mood and insists on taking everything by the wrong handle, — he is not allowed to flatter himself that he is a superior person with a "temperament," or a fine thinker with a gift for righteous indignation. He is simply set down as cross. It is presumed that he got up the wrong way, and he is advised to try again and see if he cannot do better. If he is fortunate enough to be thrown into the society of his contemporaries, he is subjected to a course of salutary discipline. No mercy is shown to "cross-patch." He cannot present his personal grievances to the judgment of his peers, for his peers refuse to listen. After a while he becomes conscious that his wrath defeats itself, as he hears the derisive collet:

> "Johnny's mad,
> And I am glad."

A LITERARY CHRISTMAS

What's the use of being unpleasant any longer if it only produces such unnatural gaiety in others. At last, as a matter of self-defense, he puts on the armor of good-humor which alone is able to protect him from the attacks of his adversaries.

But when a person has grown up and is able to express himself in literary language, he is freed from these wholesome restraints. He may indulge in peevishness to his heart's content, and it will be received as a sort of esoteric wisdom. For we are simple-minded creatures, and prone to superstition. It is only a few thousand years since the alphabet was invented, and the printing press is still more recent. There is still a certain Delphic mystery about the printed page which imposes upon the imagination. When we sit down with a book, it is hard to realize that we are only conversing with a fellow-being who may know little more about the subject in hand than we do, and who is attempting to convey to us not only his life-philosophy, but also his aches and pains, his likes and dislikes, and the limitations of his own experience. When doleful sounds come from the oracle, we take it for granted that something is the matter with the universe, when all that has happened is that one estimable gentleman, on a particular morning, was out of sorts when he took pen in hand.

At Christmas time, when we naturally want to be on good terms with our fellow-men, and when our pursuit of happiness takes the unexpectedly genial form of plotting for their happiness, the disposition of our favorite writers becomes a matter of great importance to us. A surly, sour-tempered person, taking advantage of our confidence, can turn us against our best friends. If he has an acrid wit he may make us ashamed of our highest enthusiasms. He may so picture human life as to make the message "Peace on earth, good will to men" seem a mere mockery.

I have a friend who has in him the making of a popular scientist, having an easy flow of extemporaneous theory, so that he is never closely confined to his facts. One of his theories is that pessimism is purely a literary disease and that it can only be conveyed through the printed page. In having a single means of infection it follows the analogy of malaria, which in many respects it resembles. No mosquito, no malaria; so no book no pessimism. Of course you must have a particular kind of mosquito and he must have got the infection somewhere; but that is his concern, not yours. The important thing for you is that he is the middleman on whom you depend for the disease. In like manner, so my friend asserts, the writer is the middle-man through whom the public gets its supply of pessimism.

I am not prepared to give an unqualified assent to this theory, for I have known some people who were quite illiterate who held very gloomy views in regard to the world in general. At the same time it seems to me there is something in it.

When an unbookish individual is in the dumps, he is conscious of his own misery, but he doesn't attribute it to all the world. The evil is narrowly localized. He sees the dark side of things because he is so unluckily placed that that alone is visible, but he is quite ready to believe that there is a bright side somewhere.

I remember several pleasant half-hours spent in front of a cabin on the top of a far western mountain. The proprietor of the cabin, who was known as "Pat," had dwelt there in solitary happiness until an intruder came and settled nearby. There was incompatibility of temper, and a feud began. Henceforth Pat had a grievance, and when a sympathetic traveler passed by, he would pour out the story of his woes; for like the wretched man of old he meditated evil on his bed against his enemy. And yet, as I have said, the half-hours spent in listening to these tirades were not cheerless, and no bad effects followed. Pat never impressed me as being inclined to misanthropy; in fact, I think he might have been set down as one who loved his fellow-men, always excepting the unlucky individual who lived next to him. He never imputed the sins of this particular person to Humanity. There was always a sunny margin of good-humor around the black object of his hate. In this respect Pat was angry and sinned not. After listening to his vituperative eloquence I would ride on in a hopeful frame of mind. I had seen the worst and was prepared for something better. It was too bad that Pat and his neighbor did not get on better together. But this was an incident which did not shut out the fact that it was a fine day, and that some uncommonly nice people might live on the other side of the range.

But if Pat had possessed a high degree of literary talent, and had written a book, I am sure the impression would have been quite different. Two loveless souls, living on top of a lonely mountain, with the pitiless stars shining down on their futile hate! What theme could be more dreary. After reading the first chapter I should be miserable.

"This," I should murmur, "is Life. There are the two symbolic figures, — Pat and the Other. The artist, with relentless sincerity, refuses to allow our attention to be distracted by the introduction of any characters unconnected with the sordid tragedy. Here is human nature stripped of all its pleasant illusions. What a poor creature is man!"

Pat and his neighbor, having become characters in a book, are taken as symbols of humanity, just as the scholastic theologians argued that Adam and Eve, being all that there were at the time, should be treated as "all mankind," at least for purposes of reprobation.

The author who is saddest when he writes takes us at a disadvantage. He may assert that he is only telling us the truth. If it is ugly that is not his fault. He pictures to us the thing he sees, and if we could free ourselves from our sentimental preference for what is pleasing we should praise him for his fidelity.

"You doubtless," says the cross wrier, "would like to have us turning out endless Christmas carols, and at regular intervals call out 'God bless Us, Every One.' It would be agreeable to you to have us adopt permanently the point of view of Scrooge when, after his melodramatic transformation, 'he went to church, and walked about the streets, and watched the people hurrying to and fro, and patted children on the head, and questioned beggars, and looked down into the kitchens of houses, and up into the windows, and found that everything could yield him pleasure.' If you think we are going to supply you with that sort of thing you are mistaken. If you want something 'strong,' or 'sincere,' or heart-rending or disillusioning we are prepared to meet you. But no more Christmas caroling, — that has gone out."

In all this the author is well within his rights. If he prefers unmitigated gloom in his representation of life, we on our part have the right of not taking him too seriously. Speaking of disillusion, two can play at that game. We must get over our too romantic attitude toward literature. We must not exaggerate the significance of what is presented to us, and treat that which is of necessity partial as if it were universal. When we are presented with a poor and shabby world, peopled only with sordid self-seekers, we need not be unduly depressed. We take the thing for what it is, a fragment. We are not looking directly at the world but only at so much of it as has been mirrored in one particular mind. The mirror is not a very large one, and there is an obvious flaw in it which more or less distorts the image. Still let us be thankful for what is set before us and make allowance for the natural human limitations. In this way one can read almost any sincere book, not only with profit but with a certain degree of pleasure.

Let us remember that only a very small amount of good literature falls within Shelley's definition of poetry as "the record of the best and happiest moments of the happiest and best minds." For these rare outpourings of joyous, healthy life we are duly thankful. They are to be received as gifts of the gods, but we must not expect too many of them. Even the best minds often leave no record of their happiest moments, while they become garrulous over what displeases them. The cave of Adullam has always been the most prolific literary centre. Every man who has a grievance is fiercely impelled to self-expression. He is not content till his grievance is published to the unheeding world. And it is well that it is so. We should be in a bad way if it were not for these inspired Adullamites who prevent us from resting in slothful indifference to evil.

Most writers of decided individuality are incited by a more or less iconoclastic impulse. There is an idol they want to smash, a convention lie which they want to expose. It is the same impulse which moves almost every right-minded citizen, once or twice in his life, to write a letter of protest to the newspaper. Things are going wrong in his neighborhood and he is impatient to set them right.

There are enough real grievances, and the full expression of them is a public service. But the trouble is that any one who develops a decided gift in that direction is in danger of becoming the victim of his own talent. Eloquent fault-finding becomes a mannerism. The original grievance loses its sharp outlines; it, as it were, passes from the solid to the gaseous state. It becomes vast, pervasive, atmospheric. It is like the London fog, enveloping all objects and causing the eyes of those who peer through it to smart.

This happened, in the last generation, to Carlyle and Ruskin, and in a certain degree to Matthew Arnold. Each had his group of enthusiastic disciples who responded eagerly to their master's call. They renounced shams or machine-made articles or middle-case Philistinism as the case might be. They went in for sincerity, or Turner, or "sweetness and light," with all the ardor of youthful neophytes. And it was good for them. But after a while they became, if not exactly weary in well-doing, at least a little weary of the unintermittent tirades against ill-doing. They were in the plight of the good Christian who goes to church every Sunday only to hear the parson rebuke the sins of the people who are not there. The man who dated his moral awakening from 'Sartor Resartus' began to find the 'Latter Day Pamphlets' wear on his nerves. It is good to be awakened; but one doesn't care to have the rising bell rung in his ears all day long. One must have a little ease, even in Zion.

Ruskin had a real grievance and so had Matthew Arnold. It is too bad that so much modern work is poorly done; and it is too bad that the middle-case Englishman has a number of limitations that are quite obvious to his candid friends, — and that his American cousin is no better.

But when all this has been granted why should one talk as if everything were going to the dogs? Why not put a cheerful courage on as we work for better things? Even the Philistine has his good points and perhaps may be led where he cannot be driven. At any rate he is not likely to be improved by scolding.

I am beginning to feel the same way even about Ibsen. Time was when he had an uncanny power over my imagination. He had the word of a disenchanter. Here, I said, is one who has the gift of showing us the thing as it is. There is not a single one of these characters whom we have not met. Their poor shifts at self-deceit are painfully familiar to us. In the company of this keen-eyed detective we can follow human selfishness and cowardice through all their disguises. The emptiness of conventional respectabilities and pieties, and the futility of the spasmodic attempts at heroism are obvious enough.

It was an eclipse of my faith in human nature. The eclipse was never total because the shadow of the book could not quite hide the thought of various men and women whom I had actually known. This formed the luminous penumbra.

After a while I began to recover my spirits. Why should I be so depressed? This is a big world and there is room in it for many possibilities of good and evil. There are all sorts of people, and their existence is no argument against the existence of quite another sort.

Let us take realism in literature for what it is and no more. It is, at best, only a description of an infinitesimal bit of reality. The more minutely accurate it is, the more limited it must be in its field. You must not expect to get a comprehensive view through high-powered microscope. The author is severely limited, not only by his choice of a subject but by his temperament and by his opportunities for observation. He is doing us a favor when he focuses his attention upon one special object and makes us see it clearly.

A LITERARY CHRISTMAS

It is when the realistic writer turns philosopher and begins to generalize that we must be on our guard against him. He is likely to use his characters as symbols, and the symbolism becomes oppressive there are some businesses which ought not to be united. They hinder healthful competition and produce a hateful monopoly. Thus in some states the railroads that carried coal also went into the business of coal-mining. This has been prohibited by law. It is held that the railroad, being a common carrier, must not be put into a position in which it will be tempted to discriminate in favor of its own products. For a similar reason it may be argued that it is dangerous to allow the dramatist or novelist to furnish us with a "philosophy of life." The chances are that, instead of impartially fulfilling the duties of a common carrier, he will foist upon us his own goods and force us to draw conclusions from the samples of human nature he has in stock. I should not be willing to accept a philosophy of life even from so accomplished a person as Mr. G. Bernard Shaw; not because I doubt his cleverness in presenting what he sees, but because I have a suspicion that there are some very important things which he does not see.

It is really much more satisfactory for each one to gather his life philosophy from his own experience rather than from what he reads out of a book or from what he sees on the stage. "The harvest of a quiet eye" is, after all, more satisfying than the occasional discoveries of the unquiet eye that seeks only the brilliantly novel.

AT CHRISTMAS TIME those of us who in our journey through the world have found some things which seem to us to be good, and which encourage us to hope for more good farther on, need not be greatly troubled by what is continually being written against our creed. For, after all, the Christmas creed is a reasonable one and keeps close to the everyday facts. It is not the assertion that there is no evil, but it is the assertion that we may overcome evil with good. Good-will is not a bit of weak sentimentalism; it is a force actively engaged in righting the wrongs it sees. A great fight has been going on; it calls for courage and endurance; but it is a good fight and we are glad that we are in it. Though it has looked desperate at times, we have the conviction that the good cause is going to win out.

When one whose business it is to report the varying phases of the world struggle describes the forces of evil with an intimacy of knowledge that is convincing, while the good is far in the background, we need not share his despondency. "What an excellent war correspondent," we say; "how faithfully he tells what he sees! What a pity it is that he follows the wrong army!"

Christmas Candy.

BY ALMA WEISNER

From 'The New Republic,' December 1906

The girl who came out from the inner office when I applied for work at the candy factory said they didn't need any packers, but that they would put me on as an inexperienced dipper. I agreed to come to work the following morning. The hours were from eight to six, with an hour for lunch and a half day on Saturday. I was to get nine dollars a week to start.

The next morning at a few minutes before eight I came to the office again. There were five other girls standing around, and as we waited we talked. One of the girls had worked in a gas mask factory where she said she had made twenty-eight dollars a week, and here she was applying for work at nine. One by one the man in the office called us to him, took our names and addresses, our age and our previous experience. He offered at first to put me in the hard candy room as a packer, but when I seemed to want to learn to dip he was glad to send me to that room, for before Christmas dippers are in demand. One of the young girls in the office showed us where to hang our hats and coats — a dark, stuffy room that smelled of chocolate, where we groped around for a hook. Then up three flights to the dipping room.

CHRISTMAS CANDY

When we came into the room the forelady ordered the first two girls to sit down at the tables. She sent me to the farther end of the room and called a tiny Italian girl, Mary, to show me how to pack. It was simple enough. All I had to do was to take a five-pound cardboard box, put a piece of wax paper on the bottom, fill in a layer of chocolates, then another piece of wax paper, then a sheet of cardboard, then wax paper, now another layer of chocolates, and repeat. For a while Mary brought me the heavy boards on which the dried chocolates were, then I had to get them myself. I stood filling five-pound boxes for two hours, then I stepped over to the Italian woman nearest me and asked her if I could get a bench and sit down to the work. She told me I could not sit down until the forelady came and told me to. So I worked on. Almost all the packers were old Italian women who stood stolidly and moved nothing but their hands, and those very quickly. I wondered how they could stand like that, without the ceaseless shifting from foot to foot which alone made the thing possible for me. At eleven o'clock the forelady came back and sent me to learn to dip. I was glad to drop to a bench in front of the long table.

Chocolate dipping is a skilled occupation. It takes all of a year to become an expert dipper. In front of me was a marble slab, to my right an oblong tin tray, with a smaller tray in front to hold the loose bits of chocolate. In the middle of the table was a narrow basin of chocolate, kept hot and fluid by electricity. I liked Celia, the girl who showed me how to dip. In the basin was a long-handled ladle, and Celia told me to pour a dipperful of the chocolate on the marble slab in front of me. I did so, and Celia put her right hand into the thick fluid and cooled it off; then she emptied it by handfuls into the tin tray at the side and told me to scrape what remained on the marble slab back into the basin. We then poured a dipperful of the warm chocolate into the back part of the tin tray to cool off. Celia told me to put my hand into the cooled chocolate on the tray. I put it in. It was like messing around in fudge, just before it is ready to pour into the pans. One of the Italian girls said, "Just suppose the 'igh brows were to see us doin' this."

A LITERARY CHRISTMAS

The first two days I was kept at dipping almonds. Celia was very good at showing me carefully just how to do it. She asked me my first name. "Sadie," I said it was. She would pat me in an encouraging way on the shoulder. She was a Spanish girl, and she wore the filthiest apron I have ever seen. Everything smelled sickeningly of the chocolate. The first day I worked there were no windows open, and there were over a hundred women in the room. Great care is needed in keeping the temperature of the dipping department just right, as the chocolate must Harden quickly. The pipes overhead were white with frost. Most of the women wore old ragged sweaters under their aprons. We all had to wear muslin caps.

At my left was a large wooden tray filled with almonds coated with sugar. With my left hand I had to throw one of the nuts into the cooled chocolate on the tin tray, cover it completely, lift it out, and place it on the board in front of me. On the board, each time I took a new one, I had to lay a piece of heavy paper, with the trademark embossed backwards on it, so that each piece of candy bore the firm's initials. To lift the covered almond out of the chocolate, I had first to find the point, play the nut upon my middle and first finger, with the point facing toward the palm of my hand, then put my thumb on the point and slide the almond from my fingers to the paper-covered board. As I put it down I had to make the "stroke" that is found on all high priced candy, by having enough of the chocolate on the end of my thumb to make the backward line on the tope of the candy, I spilled chocolate from my fingers as I tried to get the nut on the board, and the stroke was not always as perfect as it should have been. Celia was patient. She really was a good teacher.

The forelady spent most of her time among the experienced dippers. Occasionally she came to the back of the room to nag the packers. She was a fat Italian woman, made ill natured by constant speeding up of the girls. I remember that one day a few minutes before twelve some of the girls started to sing the Star Spangled Banner, and she scolded, "I don't know what youse are; youse act like a lot of loose lunatics."

175

CHRISTMAS CANDY

At twelve o'clock the bell rang. There were two dilapidated, rusty sinks in the room. There was plenty of hot water, but liquid soap at only one of the sinks. The first day I worked there was a towel at the rear of the room. It was black by noon time, and for two days it hung there; after that we either didn't try to dry our hands or else we wiped them off on the paper that was lying around. A sign over the sink said, "Bring your own drinking cup. Always wash your hands before resuming work." One of the women had a tin cup and we all borrowed it from her. The toilet arrangements were far from ideal, but when the girls came upstairs they never dared to take the time to stop and rinse their hands before going back to their places. Where the public is asked to pay an unusually high price for the product it would seem that unusual care should be taken to keep the place as clean and as decent as possible. The Y.W.C.A. is reported as calling the girls "tough," and it would be a wonder if they were anything else.

Most of the girls brought their lunch and ate it sitting around the room in which they worked. A few groups gathered and talked; most of the women sat alone and rested. We had to be back in the room at ten minutes to one, to empty the larger pan, in which the chocolate had caked, into a box at one end of the room. At one o'clock the bell rang and we started again.

The girls at my table were young, only opposite me was there an older married woman. They talked in low tones to one another. Sometimes Celia would call them down, saying, "Youse know I get scolded when you girls talk." Celia said my apron, which I had paid a dollar and sixty-nine cents for at noon, was "real neat." We worked on and on. About three o'clock the girls began to watch the time. I thought that if only about half past three we could have had ten minutes in which to stand up and stretch it would have meant so much. But that, of course, would have allowed the chocolate to harden in the pans. We had to ask permission to go downstairs or to get a drink. The forewoman kept on screaming, urging the girls to work faster. Celia helped me a lot, and we talked. She said if I kept at it and worked hard, pretty soon I'd get a raise; I'd get nine and a half dollars a week. One afternoon a good-sized mouse ran across the table, creating a great and welcome commotion.

While we dipped steadily on the girls talked, mostly about their own affairs. A little girl on the opposite side of the table from me told about her "gentleman friend." He was taken with the influenza, and when at his request she went to Bellevue Hospital to see him, he was dead. Their engagement was to have been announced at Christmas. He was seventeen, she sixteen. "He was a real fine fellow," she said. "My mother liked him, too." "Are you married, Sadie?" they asked me. "Mostly married ladies work here." The girl next me said, "Seems like we never get a full week's pay. Last week they took out for Victory Day, and now this week they take a day's pay out on everyone for the War Fund Drive; and next week comes Thanksgiving. They just take the money out of your envelope and send it to the fund, and they get all the credit. A dollar and a half out of nine dollars a week only leaves seven and a half to live on," she explained to me. The married women compared notes about their husbands, and they all talked about the husbands we unmarried ones were going to get. They talked about their children and their housekeeping, and much about the cost of living. Many of them did washing and housework after they reached home at night.

Up to four o'clock I dipped fairly well for a beginner. From four to five I grew steadily worse, and from five to six I spilled chocolate over myself and over the board. All the other girls were doing the same. One night Celia, who stood all day, said, "I wish it was five o'clock." The other girls, realizing for the first time that she too was weary, asked if she were tired. She said, "Yes," and she looked it. "I wish they would hurry up and put through that law that only lets us work until five o'clock," she sighed. And we all agreed with her. That night the forelady made all the experienced dippers stay until seven o'clock, Celia with them. The girls at first refused to stay, but the forelady screamed at them, "Youse'll stay every other night until seven; I won't make youse stay 'til ten, but 'til seven youse'll stay; and youse'll work every Saturday until six, from next week on 'til Christmas." "Where," I thought, "are the labor laws and their enforcement in this state?" That last hour was torture for us all. The lights were turned on, the shades were pulled down, and the room grew steadily colder. Only the lash of the forelady's tongue kept us at it. The girls all grumbled and said that five o'clock should be the quitting time. We did not dare watch the time too closely for fear of the forelady. There was no clock in the room, but one of us had a watch. The forelady was a wonder, the girls agreed, "she never misses anything." She was kind, too, in her way, only she did scream at the girls. When the bell rang at six o'clock we had to empty the basin of hot chocolate into the tin tray to Harden overnight, which took five minutes. Then the hundred girls had to get the thickest of the chocolate off their hands, and with only two sinks it made a mob scene around them. The forelady always scolded at how slow we were (she was as tired as we). "Don't stop to manicure your hands, ladies," she would yell at us. Then we had to take off our aprons and caps, get on our street clothes, and stand in line to ring the time clock. It was always ten minutes past six before we left the factory. They made thirty minutes on the girls' time a day, since we had to be in the room at ten minutes of eight and at ten to one.

I worked all week; I was early every morning; I never worked overtime. That Saturday was the last one o'clock day until after Christmas. On my way home I stopped and asked the price of the candy I had been dipping most of the week. It was a dollar and thirty cents a pound! Celia had told me that a fairly good dipper should dip about fifty pounds a day, or three hundred a week, for the nine dollars. When I reached him I lay down to rest for a few minutes. I smelled abominably of chocolate, my hand was numb, my fingers stiff, my nails a sight and my arm aching. I rolled around for a while trying to sleep, and couldn't. Finally I did sleep. When I woke up it was after ten o'clock. So ended my first week in a candy factory.

Christmas Cakes and Christmas Parties:

A YORKSHIRE VILLAGE SKETCH.
BY J. FAIRFAX-BLAKEBOROUGH

From 'The Living Age,' December 23, 1922

In rural England the making of the Christmas cake and the subsequent 'tastings' are both something of a religion — an integral part of the festival, and inseparable from much of its custom and tradition. For weeks agone our village ladies have compared recipes, discussed the mysteries of cake-making and baking, and flitted to and fro from one another's houses on those anxious and fateful days of egg-breaking, mixing, and stirring.

The event — for it is an event — looms large in the rural calendar, ranking in importance as it does with a birth, a funeral, a wedding, a threshing, or a pig-killing day. At stated intervals neighbors will congregate and peer, skewer in hand and with bated breath, into the recess beyond the cautiously opened oven-door. They are tense moments these, and even the most stolid, calm and collected matrons will betray more than a passing flutter of excitement. For the nonce the yet anaemic-looking cake is as a king seated upon a threatened Thorne, with his courtiers around him hoping for the best, but ever fearful that the worst may happen. Doubts, assurances, and reassurances are exchanged in whispers as the assembled ladies fan themselves with spotless white aprons, donned to do honor to the occasion.

A YORKSHIRE VILLAGE SKETCH

One might imagine that the whole Yuletide happiness of each family, together with the good name and reputation of the housewife, depended upon the success of the matter in hand. One of our old village dames once put into concrete form something of the feelings of those responsible for producing a Christmas cake. 'Some has one thing,' she whined to the vicar, 'and some has another. The Lord give us all a cross of some sort. Now there's Christmas a-coming on and I haven't got the cake made yet, and I'm sure as each year comes round I feel my cross growing heavier and my trust in the Lord growing less so far as cakes goes.'

In our village the Christmas cake may not be cut till the eve of the great festival, though the small 'taster' — made specially to know the worst — may be sampled by the anxious dames in solemn conclave, for it has no tradition or sentiment surrounding it. Final criticism and a reopening of the whole discussion in calmer frame of mind are postponed till the Christmas parties, at which those who sighed and panted, shook their heads and clasped skewers in one hand as with the other they flapped apron-borne air to their faces, can afford to laugh at what for the nonce was such a tremendously serious undertaking.

These Christmas parties are not easy to arrange. Mrs. Brown or Mrs. Jones, in the neighboring town, may invite a few friends for an evening at Yuletide without even her next-door neighbor being aware of the fact either before or after the event. Not so in our village. No sooner has Mrs. Thompson, Old Betty at the shop, Rachel Ray, Lizzie Leckonby, or any of the other village ladies fixed upon a date for entertaining their friends and the ceremonial tasting of their several cakes, than the news spreads and the days are quoted in connection with further prospective social gatherings. 'It'll be new good fixing on Wednesday i' next week, coz that's awd Mary Thompson's party night, an' Friday'll be Lizzie Leckonby's. You'll have getten an invitation, haven't you?' — and so on. We are able to do nothing in secret at Carthorne, and are bound to regulate our list of invited guests to our 'do's,' not by the capacity of the 'parlor,' the number of chairs we possess, or the maximum we can 'sit down at table' with comfort, but rather with a view to maintaining future peace, good will, and friendship among our neighbors. If we haven't a sufficient supply of knives, forks, plats, or wine glasses ... well, then we must borrow, as the other folks do at Christmas party times. In fact, most of us are so lacking in moral courage that we invite rather those who fully expect to be invited than those we are most anxious to have as guests and cake-tasters. We know full well that did we do otherwise there would be subsequent 'coolness' and 'offense-takings,' and that by some, whose pride had been wounded, we should be relegated to the sandy deserts of alienation.

Mrs. Thompson, of Rose Cottage, usually leads off the round of our village Christmas parties, each of which is pretty much a replica of the others. The little-used 'front parlor' is a sort of holy of holies, into which the parson and persons of 'quality' may be shown, but which otherwise remains hermetically sealed as the repository of the grandeur of the house — heirlooms and treasures which rest on woolly mats of divers colors and varying degrees of dampness. Early Victorian chairs, surpassingly uncomfortable, are drawn in a large circle round the fire, on which a brightly burning Yule log seems entirely unable to conquer the vault-like atmosphere of this state chamber. Front parlors at Carthorne are reserved for occasions such as these, and though there would be dire offense were 'party' guests not entertained therein, they would be a great deal more at home and comfortable in the spotless kitchens. However, tradition lays it down that Christmas parties at Carthorne shall be held in the parlor, so the encased wax fruit, the staring, stuffed owls, and the rows of framed funeral cards of every relation to three generations back are all duly dusted and decorated with greenery.

At the outset there is an unbending stiffness and adamantine frost permeating and having over the assembled guests. They have all put on their 'party manners' with their festive clothes, and, sitting very erect, are obviously restrained and weighed down by a determination to 'mind their p's and q's.' The passing round of fearsomely colored and liberally frosted Christmas cards, the collection of which has extended over many years, does little toward thawing the atmosphere, nor does the family 'albium' containing the photographs of those whose 'death-cards' adorn the walls around produce buoyant merriment or peals of ribald laughter. Up to this stage everyone is painfully 'proper.' Then, with labored apologies, Mary Thompson departs to the back regions to 'see about supper.' Chairs are forthwith drawn nearer the fire, the menfolk surreptitiously remove the antimacassars which have had a subduing influence upon them, the aforementioned party manners are speedily dropped, and by the time Mrs. Thompson bids her guests follow her to the kitchen the ice is melted and the Yuletide spirit reigns at last.

There are colored Yule candles, a cheese (with the sign of the Cross scraped upon it), mince pies, Yule cake, and pig under various disguises on the table, but the pièce de résistance — the central feature of the scheme of decoration — is the cake. It appeals less to the male guests than to the ladies, though the former feel in duty bound to make some reference to it, to ask, in much the same manner as they would inquire about a recently killed porker or bullock, 'Hoo mich diz sha weigh?' Or remark that 'It leaks a good un.' The cutting of the cake is always ceremonially performed on Christmas Eve, and its virtues and shortcomings discussed then, but the present is the real public trial, when almost every cake in the neighborhood is brought under review — the 'failers' (failures), the 'sad uns,' the 'dry uns' and 'damp uns,' those which have not been baked long enough and those which have been baked too long; the cakes which have not been kept sufficiently long and those which have 'sunk i' t' middle,' not to mention those that have been iced or otherwise ambitiously decorated. The conversation may be diverted into other channels on returning to the mortuary of a parlor, but it inevitably reverts to cakes, though by this time the men have gathered themselves into a corner of the room and, fortified with a decanter of gin, are immersed in pig-, or sheep-, or beast-talk.

The earliest suggestions of departure, conveyed in such blunt terms as: 'It's aboot time we wer' makkin' tracks fer yam,' only produces a rebuke from the hostess: 'What's the use o' talkin' like that? Sit still wi' ya; the night's young yet,' but on a reiteration of the threat, Mrs. Thompson again leaves the company, her strings of beads and locket-dangling chains jangling as she moves. 'Sha's not going to get owt else for us ti eat, is sha?' asks one of the menfolk. 'Ah can't eat na more, an' it looks as though we're goin' to be here all night.'

'She'll have gone to fettle a bit o' cake,' replies the spokesman's good lady, with undisguised discomfort at John's increasing impatience. 'Sit still an' rest content. It isn't every night in t' year you come out to a party.' 'I've had enough plum cake ti last me while next Kessamus,' persists the husband. He may have had, but he cannot escape having some more, for the wine-and-cake stage of the evening's entertainment has now arrived. There is home-made wine — gooseberry, rhubarb and elder; and port for those who prefer it — port, by the way, being held to be a teetotal drink in rural Yorkshire and quite 'genteel' for the most proper ladies. So, with handkerchiefs on their laps and a return of 'party manners,' the ladies eat their second does of cake crumb by crumb, sip their wine, and resume the never-ending discussion of this particular culinary effort and cakes in general. A respectable time having elapsed (during which one or two of the menfolk have dropped asleep), a move is made by the ladies to 'the best losing-room' upstairs, where they removed their hats and coats.

So ends the first of the Christmas parties and cake-tastings, and so begins the round. All of them are pretty similar in detail, except at some of the larger farmhouses, where there are young people and where an adjournment is made from parlor to kitchen for dancing or some of the boisterous merriment and unrestrained joy and fun which belong to the season, but which are lacking from the gatherings of the older folks in the restricted space and icy coldness of the front parlor.

A Christmas Dinner in the Bay of Biscay.

BY ANONYMOUS

From 'The Gentleman's Magazine,' December 1874

IT WAS last Christmas Day, the tablecloth was laid in the saloon of a mail steamboat, and the place was the Bay of Biscay. We left Southampton at noon on the 24th of December, 1873, and we were on our way to the Brazils, touching at Corunna, Caril, and Lisbon. Twelve hours before embarkation I had no more idea of spending Christmas Day in the Bay of Biscay than of sending up my plate for roast beef at the North Pole. In fact, my bachelor friends without domestic ties were invited, and had accepted the invitation, and with them and my wife and little ones I intended to dine and spend the evening of the twenty-fifth in strict accordance with tradition and national taste.

The reality was very different. "We want you, Mr. P—, to go to Lisbon and Madeira, and to do there whatever is required to ensure the speedy transmission of our correspondence from the Gold Coast. The mail steamer leaves Southampton tomorrow at twelve." These were my sudden and unchallengeable instructions, and thus it was that I found myself sitting down to dinner in the midst of the Bay of Biscay at five o'clock on the 25th day of last December.

We were a melancholy part. It was not the roughness of the sea or the motion of the ship. There was not a bit of a swell on. As smooth as landsman's heart could desire were the waters of that dreaded four hundred miles of open ocean between Ushant and Ortegal. Our boat was as steady as a castle. There was no cause of discomfort on board. Indeed we should have been thankful for a little hardship. Our grievance, I think, was the delusive decoration of the saloon with holly, the menu of roast turkey, plum pudding, and mince pies — the hollow mockeries of an old English Christmas dinner at home — so well intended by steward and cook. These things taunted us of the unlucky destiny which sent us into the middle of the lonely seas to spend our Christmas night. They set us picturing the dear family circles from which we had run away. We took our places one and all without speaking a word. The captain, at the head of the table, wore the pensive air of a family man. Two "exploiters" bound for the Brazils had been roughened by hard experience, but they were touched in a tender part at this moment of sitting down to Christmas dinner in the midst of strangers on the desolate seas. Two engineers from Yorkshire, who had been cheerfulness itself till now, were suddenly mute as fishes.

Presently, when the fish, which we had just managed to taste, was taken away, and the turkey was being handed round, a Brazilian-bound stranger made a desperate attempt to force a conversation.

"Thinking of the children, I suppose," said he to the captain.

"Haven't got any," replied the captain, with pensive gravity.

Never was a failure more signal. The well-meaning inquirer gave it up, and gain silence reigned supreme. There was nothing to fix the attention upon but the slight creaking of the ship and the swaying of the glass-rack over the table. The turkey would not go down, for every one of us had a lump in the throat less digestible than anything the steward could give us.

When the few words which had been uttered had passed almost out of recollection, and we were all mentally hundreds of miles away, the captain added, in the same serious and semi-tragical air: —

"I've got some little nephews and nieces, though," by way of explaining that he understood the tone of mind of his guests, and was not altogether outside the range of sympathy.

It was just when the plum pudding made its appearance, and when our young children should have been clapping their little hands round our tables, that an awful discovery was made. There were just thirteen of us at dinner!

Darker grew and deeper the silence and the gloom.

But the subject was in a manner congenial. Here was dismal ground on which we could all meet. The captain began to tell stories of what had occurred within his own experience, and what his father before him had told of the events associated with the sitting down of that unlucky number at table, more especially on a great day like this in the calendar. Such was the impression, I honestly avow, of those stories upon my mind, that when some months afterwards I saw on the London newspaper placards "Wreck of a Royal Mail Steamer," I found myself saying — "Ah, that must be our unlucky boat." I am glad to say my prevision was wrong; but the lost vessel was one belonging to the same house.

My own poor little contribution to the melancholy batch of superstitious recollections was derived from an occasion when a dozen of us were dining at an hotel at Bath, and a thirteenth unexpectedly arrived — a gentleman known and much esteemed by the twelve. "Here comes the victim," was the remark made as the thirteenth man sat down — and within three months that thirteenth man was dead. Now, I had never heard that the last arrival was necessarily the victim, and I was endeavoring to remove any particularly pointed application of the narrative by the well-worn argument that out of a general company of thirteen middle-aged men it was not so very unlikely that one might die in the course of twelve months, irrespective of the magic potency of fatal numbers; but somehow my philosophy did not mend the matter. After all, the idea was not absolutely exhilarating that the chances might be in favor of at least one of this small party dying before Christmas Day, 1874. Pondering woefully on this point, I glanced surreptitiously towards the seat which had been occupied by the guest who had been the thirteenth to sit down to this saloon dinner — and the place was vacant. The circumstances of the hour had been nearly enough for every one of us; the story of the thirteenth finished the Christmas dinner of 1873 for him. He lived three days longer, to my certain knowledge, and I trust he is good for a far happier dinner on the twenty-fifth of this present month; but it must be admitted that the odds on that mournful day were against him.

Dinner was over, but we could not say we had dined. The pudding had been tasted for the sake of "the children," but we were glad when it was all over. The passengers, one by one, slunk away almost unobserved to their berths. No one made the attempt even to appear cheerful. I believe I could have worked myself into a something resembling placid enjoyment of a cigar on deck with the genial Irish doctor, but just then, as he told me, we were steaming very near the spot where the London went down!

This was too much for one Christmas day, and I gave it up, and went off like the rest to my cabin to mix up in dreams the thirteenth arrival at dinner, the children, and the wreck of the London.

It is astonishing how cheerful we all were next morning. We had got over Christmas day, and had run through the Bay and were ploughing along joyfully at the rate of twelve knots off the coast of Spain. Not one of us on board, I think, would have exchanged places on that Boxing Day with those dyspeptic fiends at home whose too cheerful spirits had so haunted us the day before. We were braced up and renewed for the business, full of interest and novelty, that lay before most of us. But if the fates will let me eat my Christmas dinner at home in this current December I expect some sort of recompense in double merriment for that melancholy dinner hour in the Bay of Biscay on the twenty-fifth of December, 1873.

www.ingramcontent.com/pod-product-compliance
Lightning Source LLC
Chambersburg PA
CBHW020637180626
46816CB00003B/1016